THE
THREE
STOOGES
Book of Scripts

Volume II

THE THREE STOOGES
Book of Scripts

Volume II

by
Joan Howard Maurer
and
Norman Maurer

CITADEL PRESS • Secaucus, New Jersey

Library of Congress Cataloging-in-Publication Data

Maurer, Joan Howard.
  The Three Stooges book of scripts.

  Vol. 1 includes film scripts of "You nazty spy"
(1940), "Three little pigskins" (1934), and "Man in
black" (1934); v. 2 includes scripts of Restless
Knights, We want our mummy, and Yes, we have no bonanza.
  1. Three Stooges films.   I. Title.
PN1995.9.T5M38   1984   791.43'75   84-17614
ISBN 0-8065-0933-3 (v. 1)
ISBN 0-8065-1018-8 (v. 2)

Published by Citadel Press
A division of Lyle Stuart Inc.
120 Enterprise Ave., Secaucus, N.J. 07094
In Canada: Musson Book Company
a division of General Publishing Co. Limited
Don Mills, Ontario

Queries regarding rights and permissions should be
addressed to: Lyle Stuart, 120 Enterprise Avenue,
Secaucus, N.J. 07094

Manufactured in the United States of America

To Michael, Jeffrey, Sonya and Margana
whose affinity for life has
helped make our lives more real,
enabling us to communicate better
with the world around us.

CONTENTS

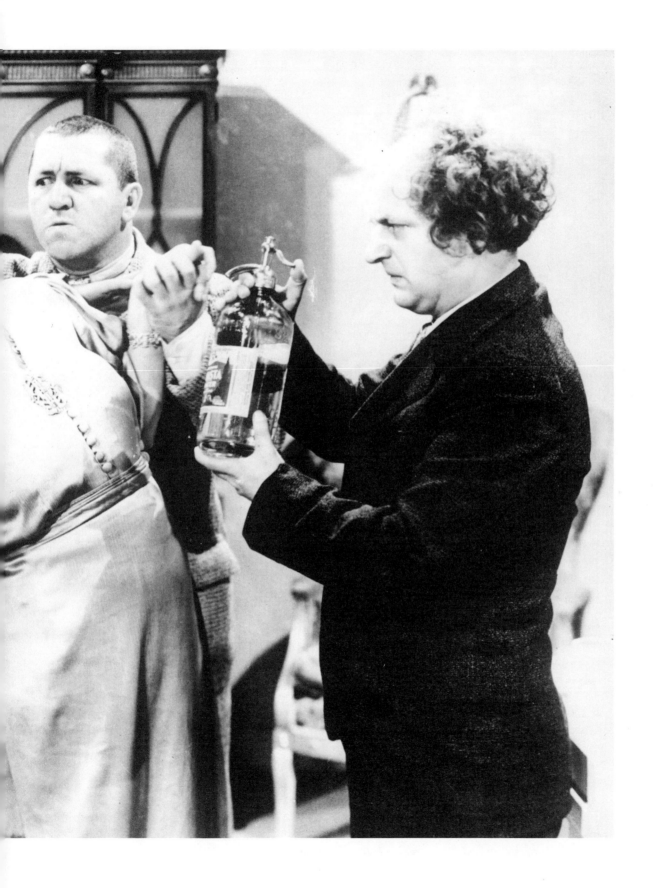

ACKNOWLEDGMENTS

M. Agrelius

Joel Appell

Loel Barr

Lester Borden and Columbia Pictures

Joe Caruso

Leslie Carvell

Chicago Tribune

Jim Cohen

Comedy Magazine

Dennis Daniel, Prod. Dir. WBAB

Hollis Davids

Dennis Doph

Jim Davis and *Nine Lives of Garfield*

Archer Dusablon

Margaret Engel

Tony Franco

S.G.

Janet Gamble

George Gately, *Heathcliff* and McNaught Synd.

Jeff Gilmore

Whoopi Goldberg

Alan Hashimoto

Jim Healy

Rev. Kenneth R. Heath

Richard Hoover

Michael Jackson

Ted Key and *Hazel*

King Features Syndicate

Wayne Koch

Searle Kramer

George Kulovitz

Charles Lamont

Bob Lancaster

Jean Lichtenstein

Leonard Maltin

Margaret Herrick Library's staff at the Academy of Motion Picture Arts and Sciences

Stanley Marx

Mack Mattingly, Augusta Chronicle

Mike Modejeski

Caspar Monahan

Dennis Newman

Ellie Padell

Mike Peters, *Mother Goose and Grimm*

Tribune Media Services

Jayne Rockmill

Michael Russo

Norman Shubert

Bill Spicer

Texas Monthly

Bruce Torrence, Historical Collection

Sam Viviano, New York Daily News

Robin Wagner

Mark Wanamaker, Bison Archives

Mike Weston

Belita Provenza William

Tom Wilson, *Ziggy* and Universal Press Synd.

Writer's Computer Store-Dan and Gabriele

Thomas Zappulla

Allan Wilson, my editor

Lyle and Carole Stuart, my publishers

And finally, to my father for being a saver—of everything—who ignored the printed ultimatum on each Columbia screenplay which read: "Please return this script at once to mimeograph department when you are finished with same."

FOREWORD
by
Whoopi Goldberg

What wonderful memories I have of the Stooges. When I was growing up watching them it was like the great escape to a place where one could laugh. I remember coming home from school in New York City and turning on Channel 11 with officer Joe Bolton. Man! The whole evening for me was set on the Stooges. Bits like the skeleton coming out of the trunk and having Larry say, "Look—Red Skeleton" —the best!

My brother—who was older and cooler—also watched their comedies and lost his cool many a time watching as did my mother. I guess, deep down, Mom was also a Stooges fan and I was allowed to enjoy them without any interference. And I remember my cool brother, who was six years older, always seemed to be funnier and looser after watching Larry, Moe and Curly do their wacky routines.

Today, I hear some people say that the Stooges' comedy is violent, but their violence, if you can call it that, is fun and hysterically funny; sorta like an animated cartoon with real people. My mom enjoyed watching them along with me and often talked about their comedy because it is ageless.

As a child, I had a crush on Moe. It sounds crazy but no one ever explained to me that the comedies I was seeing were filmed before I was born. Then, later, I fell hard for Larry and then even harder for Curly! I used to imitate him all the time. It's so great, that Nyuk Nyuk Nyuk of his. Now my daughter knows where it came from also. And the two of us laugh together. Ehhh! Ehhh! Ehhh!

Now that I'm a grown woman and in show business, I still watch Stooge comedies and am more aware than ever of their incredible timing which has had a great effect on me. Studying their antics, I learned how to fall down and not get hurt, how to take and react to physical comedy. Their timing was precision. They were like dancers or great mimes.

What I liked as a kid and still admire about the Stooges was their slapstick precision: the sound effects, the comedy bits, the silly songs, all of it. God! They were so in tune, like clockwork. They had the amazing timing which you'd expect more from a duo than a trio. Their takes, movements—I studied their routines and many of them gave me great ideas for my own work.

And look at them today—cult heroes. And you say, Why? It's because (a) They're funny. (b) They're great. (c) They're timeless.

I realize now that names are important to success. A bald man named Curly. That was funny. I recall looking for a name myself and how nine years ago while working at the San Diego Repertory Theatre, doing "A Christmas Carol," I found myself talking with friends about names we'd never name our children— like Bang, Whoosh, Slash. Then someone said, "A great name for you'd be Whoopi." And it stuck—in a big way.

Ever since I can remember, I knew that comedy and acting would be my thing. And as I grew up and watched John Garfield, Spencer Tracy, Zasu Pitts, Diana Sands and the Three Stooges, the feeling became stronger.

The Stooges, along with Lenny Bruce, Lord Buckley, Moms Mabley and Richard Pryor, made me pay attention to comedy, and from a very straight theatre trip I began to integrate comedy and theatre.

And as my career moved through these many phases, I recall being very secure with the Stooges, certain that they'd be three cats I could talk to, three cats who would always make me laugh no matter how many times I saw the same bit.

There are so many things, so many ways that watching the Stooges has helped me, and I only wish they were here to see what their humor has spawned in me.

To me and to millions of others who grew up weaned on their comedies, the Stooges were something special. As a kid I would just crack up at their incredible, zany antics. Today, as a professional, I marvel at what they achieved in their lengthy, fifty-year career.

To have created such memorable and imitable comedy on such low budgets is a miracle in itself. To have sustained and kept generation after generation laughing for over half a century is not a miracle but concrete proof of their professionalism and the timeless quality of their special form of slapstick comedy.

These were three cats who made over 200 films that have withstood the test of time and will undoubtedly continue to entertain audiences far into the future.

Who knows. One day, E.T.'s grand-kids on some distant planet could be just like me when I was a kid. . . rushing home from school to watch syndicated re-runs of the Three Stooges.

And so, on behalf of all future grand-kids and me, thank you with all my heart, Moe, Larry and Curly.

WHOOPI GOLDBERG

PREFACE

My vast assortment of Three Stooges memorabilia is at last in a neat, safe, womb-like location—a far cry from the state it was in when I was working on *Book of Scripts—Volume I*. During that time, I had to wend my way up to our attic via a rickety ship's ladder that telescoped down from the ceiling in our hall. To get from my office to my vast assortment of research material and the chaotic mish-mash of odds and ends surrounding it was a nightmare. Luggage, clothing, old baskets, gift boxes—you name it and you'd find it in our attic.

While writing the *Curly* book, not only was this cavernous storage room a disaster area, but I was also going through the turmoil of a major remodeling of my bedroom and bath. Both of these rooms had to be emptied, and because of this, even more things were tossed into an already over-crowded space.

Now, wonder of wonders, this same attic has been remodeled and what a pleasure it is to have everything neat and clean and at my fingertips.

All this longed-for cleanliness and organization must have gotten to me, for I immediately ran out to the Writer's Computer store and bought myself a word-processor/computer in-

tending to use it on my next writing endeavor. Dan and Gabriele, the owners of the store, had the patience of saints, and helped bring this slow-learner into the mysterious world of PC's and megabytes.

While playing with my new toy, I came up with an idea for what I thought would be the perfect book to put into it—which by the way had nothing to do with the Stooges. I suppose I wanted to prove that I could write about something other than my father and his partners.

With an assortment of exciting new ideas churning about in my head, I flew to San Francisco to the American Booksellers Convention to pitch this new book concept to my publishers, Lyle and Carol Stuart. I barely got out the words, "I have an idea for another book," when Lyle stopped me and said, "Speaking of books, I've made a decision. I'd like you to write, *Three Stooges Book of Scripts—Volume II*.

Although disappointed that my first, non-Stooge book would have to be temporarily shelved, I was delighted to learn that Volume I had proved to be successful enough to warrant a sequel.

In the first volume of *Book of Scripts*, al-

The author's attic BEFORE remodel.

though chronology was considered, I felt that my script choices should have more to do with subject matter than with what date the shorts were produced. The choices were based on comedy, fun and visual impact and included *Men in Black, Three Little Pigskins, Punch Drunks, You Nazty Spy* and the comedy routine, *Niagara Falls.*

However, for Volume II, I decided to make my script choices for other reasons. I thought it would be of interest to fans and film buffs alike to be able to follow a Three Stooges script at the same time they watched it on television. Consequently, I searched through RCA/Columbia's library of Three Stooges video cassettes. After looking at the available tapes, I chose the cassette with the three films which I felt would be fun, would be visual and have enough action to fit into our plans of pulling frames from the films to illustrate the book.

The end of my search was Volume IX of the Stooge tapes, which consisted of *Restless Knights, We Want Our Mummy,* and *Yes, We Have No Bonanza.* To fill out the book, I decided to include a chapter on their most successful film, the 1962 feature *The Three Stooges Meet Hercules.*

Although a history of the Stooges was written in one form or another in all the Stooge books, I felt a need to include a mini one in this book.

As I did in the first *Book of Scripts,* I decided again to sacrifice photographic quality for photographic fun and blow up the actual 35mm frames from the films. Thanks to Columbia Pictures and Lester Borden, pristine prints of my choices were ordered and sent on to me.

At Columbia Studios in Burbank, I went about the job of selecting frames for illustrating the book. This time my surroundings were a world apart from the shoddy editing quarters that I was provided with when I selected frames for *Book of Scripts—Volume I.* On *Book of Scripts—Volume II,* I was able to create in luxury. When choosing frames for Volume I, I was given an old Moviola editing machine to work with and sweated it out for weeks in a closet-sized room. I was constantly breaking film and straining my eyes, trying to make my selections from a screen the size of a postage stamp. For this book, thanks to the kindness of Joel Appell, the current head of the Trailer Department at Columbia, I was given a large airy room and was allowed to use the top-of-the-line in editing equipment, an electronic wonder called the Kem. No more Moviola foot pedal with its jumpy stops and starts which led to a constant breakage of film. Selecting and marking frames was now a pleasure, with a large viewing screen that made me feel I was watching Cinemascope.

All the editors were friendly—from Dennis Newman, who was a good sport about my using a corner of his office, to Norman Schubert, who helped me thread the Kem. Joel Appell, who has the fascinating job of supervising the editing of trailers for all of Columbia Pictures product, not only gave me permission to use the editing equipment but took an active interest in what I was doing and came up with a copy of the magazine *Texas Monthly* whose cover photograph of the Three Stooges appears in the chapter "More Respect."

In this chapter on respect, I've included all the Stooge accolades that came about after 1984, and which culminated in the Stooges being honored at the Academy of Motion Picture Arts and Sciences by Columbia Pictures, who donated all 190 prints of the Three Stooges' comedies to the archives at the University of California at Los Angeles. It was a night to remember—a gala affair at the Academy's sumptuous theatre in Beverly Hills that concluded with the Mayor of Los Angeles proclaiming October 25, 1985, as Three Stooges Day.

The never-ending tributes to the Stooges from these and other sources and the warm thank-you letters from fans for sharing with them my father's memorabilia have given me the impetus to keep the Three Stooges library growing with this my fourth book about these timeless comedians.

12   *The author's attic AFTER remodel. Voila! The THREE STOOGES ATTIC MUSEUM.*

AUTHOR'S NOTE

For those readers who are not familiar with the vernacular of the motion picture screenplay and its strange language of "PANS," "DISSOLVES," "FADES," and "WIPES," I have included an annotated script page, a glossary of additional film terms and a copy of an actual cast sheet.

The reader should also be aware that, unlike those of their features, the scripts for all Stooge shorts had nothing but a production number printed on their apple-green covers.

Their humorous titles were tacked on later, many times at the eleventh hour as everyone rushed madly to get the picture to preview.

Each member of the cast and the key people in the crew would be given a final draft script, along with a mimeographed copy of the show's shooting schedule which indicated the number of days filming would take, the start and completion dates, a list of the scenes to be shot and who would be in the respective scenes.

GLOSSARY OF ADDITIONAL FILM TERMS

FADE IN: Is a scene that gradually appears at the start of every film since Edison invented the movie camera.

SHOT: Filmed sequence.

EXT: Exterior location.

INT: Interior location.

CLOSE-UP: The camera is close to an individual or an object.

LONG SHOT: The camera is some distance from the person or object; usually shows the whole body.

GROUP SHOT: A Med. Shot of a group—in our case the Stooges.

FULL SHOT: The whole scene.

INSERT: A close shot of "something" (e.g., photo, newspaper headline, telephone number) is "inserted" into the scene.

DISSOLVE TO: A slow change of scene.

WIPE TO: A trick (optical) change of scene.

FADE OUT: The picture fades away to black. A writer's dream! His work and the picture are completed.

DOLLY: A low, mobile platform which rolls on wheels to move camera about the set.

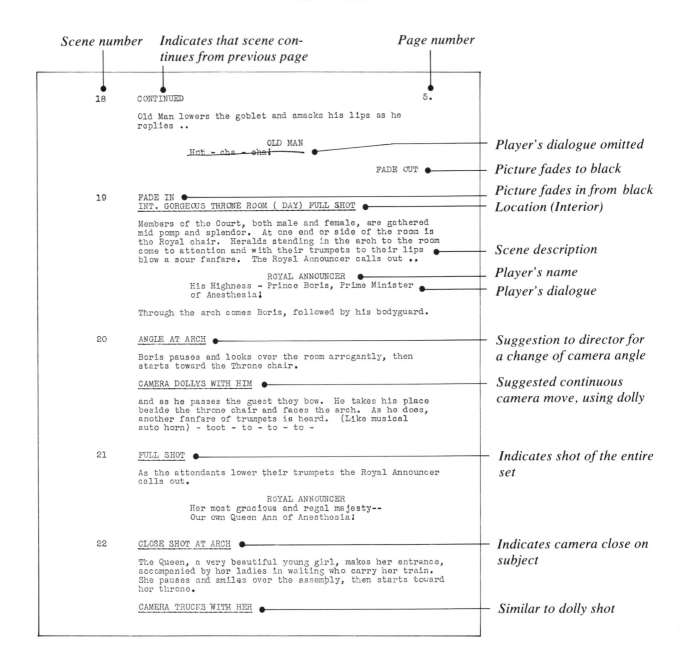

Scene number   Indicates that scene continues from previous page   Page number

18   CONTINUED   5.

Old Man lowers the goblet and smacks his lips as he replies ..

         OLD MAN

Hot - cha - cha!   — Player's dialogue omitted

       FADE OUT   — Picture fades to black

19   FADE IN   — Picture fades in from black

INT. GORGEOUS THRONE ROOM (DAY) FULL SHOT   — Location (Interior)

Members of the Court, both male and female, are gathered mid pomp and splendor. At one end or side of the room is the Royal chair. Heralds standing in the arch to the room come to attention and with their trumpets to their lips blow a sour fanfare. The Royal Announcer calls out ..   — Scene description

       ROYAL ANNOUNCER   — Player's name
     His Highness - Prince Boris, Prime Minister
     of Anesthesia!   — Player's dialogue

Through the arch comes Boris, followed by his bodyguard.

20   ANGLE AT ARCH   — Suggestion to director for a change of camera angle

Boris pauses and looks over the room arrogantly, then starts toward the Throne chair.

CAMERA DOLLYS WITH HIM   — Suggested continuous camera move, using dolly

and as he passes the guest they bow. He takes his place beside the throne chair and faces the arch. As he does, another fanfare of trumpets is heard. (Like musical auto horn) - toot - to - to - to -

21   FULL SHOT   — Indicates shot of the entire set

As the attendants lower their trumpets the Royal Announcer calls out.

       ROYAL ANNOUNCER
     Her most gracious and regal majesty--
     Our own Queen Ann of Anesthesia!

22   CLOSE SHOT AT ARCH   — Indicates camera close on subject

The Queen, a very beautiful young girl, makes her entrance, accompanied by her ladies in waiting who carry her train. She pauses and smiles over the assembly, then starts toward her throne.

CAMERA TRUCKS WITH HER   — Similar to dolly shot

Restless Knights *script.*

ASSOCIATION OF MOTION PICTURE PRODUCERS, INC.
5504 Hollywood Blvd.

COLUMBIA STUDIO   January 17th, 1935.

CALL BUREAU CAST SERVICE

"RESTLESS KNIGHTS"

Director   Charles Lamont

Moe   Moe Howard
Jerry   Jerry Howard
Larry   Larry Fine
Queen   Geneva Mitchell

BITS

Father   Walter Brennan
Count Boris   George Baxter
Announcer   Chris Franke
Wrestler   James Howard
Wrestler   Bud O'Neill
Captain of Guard   Stanley Blystone
Bit Guard   Jack Duffy
Henchman   Ernie Young
Bit Men: Lynton Brent
                            Bob Burns
                            William Irving
                            Joe Perry
                            Al Thompson
                            Bert Young
                            Dutch Hendrian
Double   George Speer
Attendant   Billy Francy
Bit Women: Marie Wells
                            Eadie Adams
                            Corinne Williams
                            Dorothy King
                            Patty Price

BB

Photocopy of actual Columbia Cast sheet for the film Restless
Knights

A Mini-History of the "Stooges"
(1922-1934)

Moe, Larry and Curly with a young Columbia Pictures starlet.

Ted Healy and his "Racketeers" in a scene from Fox's Soup to Nuts.

The evolution of the comedy team which was later to become famous as the Three Stooges began in 1922 when Moe Howard and his brother Shemp joined comedian Ted Healy (Moe's boyhood friend) as part of Healy's vaudeville act. They performed as Healy's "stooges" until 1925 when Larry Fine, the mop-topped stooge, joined the group. From that time, Ted Healy and His Stooges (also known as "Ted Healy and His Gang," "Ted Healy and His Southern Gentlemen" and "Ted Healy and His Racketeers") became headliners on top vaudeville circuits across the country. Under contract to Healy, the Stooges played in Shubert shows on Broadway and in the 1930's Fox film *Soup to Nuts*. In 1932, Shemp Howard left the act for a more promising offer from Vitaphone and the youngest member of the Howard tribe, Jerome, nicknamed "Curly," took his place.

Shemp, Moe and Larry.

Clipping, "Howard Brothers and Larry Fine."

The Messrs Shubert *present*
The Sensational Musical Comedy Revue

At an engagement at the New Yorker Cafe in early 1933 an MGM scout watched the insane, knockabout Stooges and their straight man, Ted Healy, and immediately signed them to a Hollywood contract. Healy, as usual, signed for himself as well as for the Stooges and continued to take home the lion's share of the pay, giving the Stooges their meager $150 a week.

The year at MGM was a frantic one. The Stooges starred in five shorts and had important roles in many major productions. However, midway through the year they started showing signs of discontent brought about by (among other things) their unfair treatment by Healy in regard to finances. But, caught up in the momentum of production on their current film, *Meet the Baron*, they bided their time.

In 1934, Moe finally found the courage to take an important step at the crossroads of his career which later proved to be his most singular decision. He and his stooge partners severed their long relationship with Ted Healy, struck out on their own and signed a one-picture contract with Columbia Pictures . . . a one-picture contract that lasted for twenty-five years and 190 films.

The Stooges, a "Motley" crew, in a clipping from the Detroit News.

Harry Cohn menaced by his Three Stooges.

A day on the set in Cohn's Kingdom

Columbia Pictures' Stage 3, 1935.

In 1935, the Stooges had been at Columbia for one year and already had four shorts under their belts: *Woman Haters, Punch Drunks, Men in Black* and *Three Little Pigskins*.

Harry Cohn, the head of Columbia, was thrilled; his newly acquired Stooges had found an audience. Little did he know that fifty years later that audience would be numbered in the multi-millions.

In order to bring to light a bit more data on Cohn's Kingdom and avoid duplicating the information in *Book of Scripts—Volume I,* I thought it might be interesting to know what it was like on the set during the making of one of the Stooges' comedies and to discover how the cast and crew at Columbia reacted to working with these three zany characters.

To learn how the average day began during the filming of this mayhem, I was fortunate to make contact with Mae Hershon, a script supervisor, who worked throughout the forties on many of the Stooges' shorts. Mae made me aware that working on comedies was not always a load of laughs. She should know; the script supervisor must see all, hear all and know all.

Mae explained that because the comedies had low budgets and short shooting schedules

Columbia Studios, 1438 N. Gower, Hollywood—1935.

there was a great deal of pressure during the filming of the Stooges' two-reelers. If somebody along the way blew a line or blew a special effect or just plain blew it, it could hold up the entire cast and crew. Because of this, it was imperative to be on schedule, and so the pressure would continually build. If there were any delays, then it became necessary to make up for lost time. "If you weren't careful," Mae pointed out, "you could be blamed for causing the delay even though you were perfectly innocent."

To illustrate Mae's point, I recall a story my father once told me about one of his directors who dearly loved pretty young women and would promise them parts in the comedies. Usually, they had no acting ability and trying to get a passable performance from one of them would take hours. Later, when a short went over schedule, the director would blame the Stooges.

Although Curly was not a good study, he rarely caused any sizeable delays. This cherubic stooge was a comic genius and, if he blew a line, he'd quickly improvise a hilarious bit of

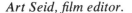

Art Seid, film editor.

insanity and the missed line would go unnoticed. Larry and Moe were constantly improvising comedic bits of dialogue (from old jokes or from vaudeville) which they'd toss in and, very often with almost no rehearsal, come up with a classic routine that remained in the film. Oftentimes this ad-libbing turned out to be funnier than the lines in the script.

Lodge Cunningham, the Stooges' sound man on several of the shorts in the early years, recalled what he observed on the set during the making of these classic scenes. Lodge was not only a personal friend of Moe's (they had the mutual hobby of stamp collecting) but he dearly loved the Stooges. According to Lodge, as he sat at his sound console, earphones in place, he would listen to the comedy which took place offstage. Luckily, many of these behind-the-camera events never made it to the silver screen. Lodge went on to explain: "For example, if Jules White's brother, Jack White, was the director and Jules had on his producer's hat, it was like a three-ring circus—with constant disagreement going on between producer, director and the Stooges."

Film frame from Stooges comedy Back from the Front. *L. to r., 1st row—Jules White; unknown bit player; Lodge Cunningham, soundman; another bit player. 2nd row—Bud Jamison.*

Harry Cohn, Columbia's "King Cohn," 1934.

Lodge continued: "In the first ring was Jules and propman Ray Hunt who constantly growled and grumbled between themselves—but loved every minute of it. Then Jules would lock horns with his brother Jack—an act in itself. While in the third ring the Stooges would be arguing among themselves as to what was the best way to do a particular scene."

I was never able to be objective like Lodge; for some reason, I was always nervous when I watched my father on stage or in front of the camera. I recall going to the set in 1935 during the making of *Hoi Polloi*. As I stood off-camera next to my father, I held my breath as he held a cream puff in each hand and prepared to throw them as soon as the director yelled, "Action." Dad was famous for his uncanny accuracy at hurling objects, a skill he had honed to perfection in his childhood, and he always threw the pies or whatever object was to be tossed when he wasn't in a scene. Even though I knew he was a crack shot, I was always uptight and worried for him, realizing that precious time would be wasted if his cream puff or pie missed its mark and the mess had to be cleaned up before shooting could resume.

I can still remember the moment as if I witnessed it yesterday. The leading lady, Grace Goodall, stood up at the head of a very elegant banquet table. The scene called for her to laugh loudly with her mouth wide open. My dad was next to Del Lord, the director, who gave my father his instructions, asking him to throw a cream puff directly into Miss Goodall's mouth. On the set, the butler was standing behind Miss Goodall and would then say, "disgusting" and turn around. After which Dad was supposed to nail him on the back of his neck with the other cream puff. This time Moe's incredible accuracy led to problems. The cream puff hit Grace squarely in the mouth leaving her gasping for breath. Unfortunately, some of the cream had gone down her windpipe and Del, concerned about her, found it necessary to call the set doctor. More than an hour passed before our leading lady was herself again, and then the shooting resumed as though nothing had happened. All in a days work on a Three Stooges comedy.

When the scene ended, everyone broke for lunch and I had a chance to look around at what went on behind the camera. A glance up at the ceiling into the scaffolding and at the reverse sides of the prop walls and all your illusions about this being an elegant dining

Soundman Lodge Cunningham being fitted for headphones (1941). Back row—L. to r., George Cooper, Eddie Bernds, John Lividary, Eddie Hahn. Front Row—Man from Western Electric and Lodge Cunningham.

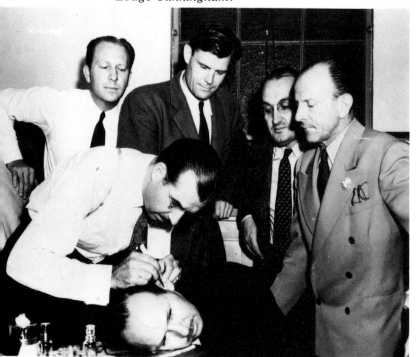

room in a posh residence vanished. The people at the table were actors, the windows of the dining room looked out over nothing but a

The Stooges waiting for the cameras to roll on the set of Termites of 1938.

giant kleig light which was there to simulate the sun, the walls were nothing more than painted and papered plywood.

One's illusions were further destroyed at the sight of webs of heavy, electrical conduit draped and coiled on every square inch of the stage floor; you took your life in your hands if you didn't watch every step. Behind the camera were more huge lights and director's chairs were scattered about for the directors and members of the cast. If you lacked status you had to sit on an "apple box"—a rectangular-shaped object which had more uses on a set than a paper clip.

There were rafters overhead which must have been three stories high, and when a scene was actually being shot, one could see dozens of men scurrying about up in the catwalks amidst a profusion of lights which came in every size and shape.

The thing that stands out in my mind as I reminisce is the heat that radiated from all the lights. If you happened to be working in the front of the camera you felt as though you would melt. Although the set always seemed to be in a state of chaotic confusion, everyone there had a job and each one seemed to know

*Moe and Curly wait for the director to shout,
"Action!" on the set of* The Sitter Downers *(1937).*

there studying them. One time I recall joining him and I remember the editor was there, making notes and watching for slow spots that he would have to repair in his cutting room.

Art Seid, a talented film editor and one of the more loyal members of Cohn's kingdom, recalled with sadness the passing on of the "good old days." "I liked the closeness—and the feeling that you weren't just working for anybody. There was always togetherness and the desire to make the best show you could," Seid explained.

"The film, before it is edited, is a cold thing," he continued. "It is up to the editor to make the action work. It was really tough to

*A serious Curly takes direction from director Jules
White.*

exactly what to do and when to do it—even the Stooges.

Moe, always serious, was constantly thinking about the upcoming scene and trying to figure out ideas to embellish them; Curly, the lackadaisical one, could be found playing cards after one scene and dozing off after the next, but when the assistant-director called his name, there he was, Johnny-on-the-spot. Larry was a "live-wire." When not performing in front of the camera, he could be found kibbitzing, laughing and telling jokes. But he did have one failing; he was the cry-baby of the group. If a slap was too hard, he'd actually cry out as though he were mortally wounded, but five minutes later he'd be laughing and back telling jokes as though nothing had happened. When they were finally ready to shoot again, the director would have the Stooges run through the scene to make sure that everything was in order. If there were special effects—and there usually were—they had to be absolutely certain that all of the actors hit their marks with precision. If a can of paint was rigged to spill or an explosion was to be triggered, it was imperative that you were in the exact spot required or there could be a massive, time-consuming clean-up job—to say nothing of possible injuries.

That same evening, all interested parties would watch the "dailies," which were the scenes shot the day before. Although Curly and Larry rarely were interested enough to watch "dailies," my father would always be

put a Stooge film together. In the early days, during the making of these comedies, everyone failed to realize the importance of scene matching. When you go from a full shot to a close-up, you're supposed to do the same thing and be in the same place. But the spontaneity and craziness of the Stooges made it almost an impossibility."

He went on to tell me how important it was to understand a comedian's style in order to edit for him. "Film is very different from TV," Art said. "In the early days of the Stooge comedies, we would edit and space for laughs. The editor would have to know what length to pause for each of the Stooges' gags so the next dialogue would not be drowned out by the audience's laughter."

Another aspect of the Stooge comedies that stands out in my mind were the sneak previews of their shorts. When I was in my teens, I recall going to see several of these previews, which were always held on a Friday night. The film was rushed out to the preview theatre, which was usually in a small outlying community away from Hollywood. And it was there, after noting the audience's reactions, that the editors, in a conference with the Stooges and the director, made their final decisions on the timing and the final cut of the film.

Art Seid told me: "Curly was easy . . . all I had to do was leave plenty of space for laughs. Larry was timed tight, as he was given very few funny lines. Moe had to have plenty of space for his reactions, as he'd always come up with his silly looks and grimaces."

During my visits to the set, I came to realize that as good as Jules White was as a director, the Stooges did not enjoy working with him. The reasons were clear. Jules himself admitted to being "The Fourth Stooge" and always acted out all the action and dialogue prior to the Stooges doing a scene. He was quite professional, but Moe, Larry and Curly were also pros and resented this heavy-handed direction.

Curly has a bit of tailoring done to his "seat" for a special effect while Shemp (far left), Moe and the crew give him support.

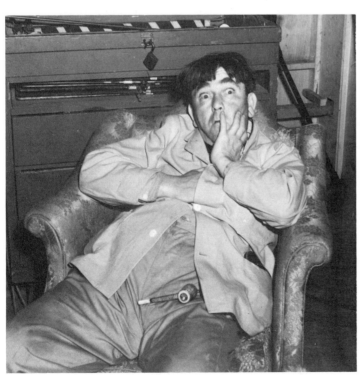

A startled Moe realizes it's time for the next take.

Art Seid expounded on the subject when he said, "Jules would say whatever he had to say from a directorial standpoint, but Moe really staged the routines and was able to speak the language of the other two Stooges. When I visited the set it was Moe who set the timing pattern." Seid went on to say, "Larry was not much of an ad-libber but when Moe and Curly started doing their crazy stuff off screen, it kept you in stitches. Then Jules would run over to them and yell, 'Save it for the cameras.' "

Mae Hershon, the script supervisor, had her own recollections of a day on the set with Jules and the Stooges: "One film we shot had an earthquake scene and the special-effects men had everything all set up so that when Jules pushed a button everything on the set would start shaking, including a goldfish bowl which was supposed to come crashing down on someone's head. Because Jules had this penchant for acting out an entire scene for cast and crew—right down to where they put their feet—he made the mistake of pushing the button during his directorial machinations. The

The author at age eight has her picture taken with the Stooges. "Ho-hum!"

prop man went into action and the whole set was demolished without the camera recording a single frame."

I can also recall other instances where I was very nervous for my father and the other two Stooges. Every time a scene was ready to be shot, I would bite off another nail. The set-ups for almost every shot were always very complicated. Besides having to know all your dialogue and that of the other actors, and having to hit your mark exactly so a special effect didn't blow up in your face, there was that precision of slapstick craziness to go through. Not to be overlooked was the studio breathing down one's neck, making sure that you met the skimpy, five-day schedule and stayed within an allocated budget. It always seemed to me to be an absolute miracle that the Stooges could do their complicated scenes in one take, but they always did.

Guests, like myself, visiting the set had a tenseness as they worried about what the director might do to you if, after they had successfully gone through a complicated scene, you coughed, sneezed or—horror of horrors—laughed and caused a retake. I very often found myself with my hand clamped over my mouth to choke back any and every possible noise. Script supervisor Mae Hershon told me that there were times when she couldn't do her job, as she'd get hysterical during a "take" and there she was, seated directly under the sound boom.

In the summer of 1985, after not having set foot on a sound stage in more than fifteen years, I had the opportunity to visit a set once again. Superstar, rock-singer Michael Jackson invited me to come over and watch him during the filming of "Captain EO," a 15-minute, $15,000,000 film for an exhibit at Walt Disney's Epcot.

Fifteen million dollars! It was hard to believe that this 15-minute Disney film was almost the same length as a Stooges short. With that kind of money Harry Cohn could have made 600 Stooges comedies.

The cost of filming has come a long way from the Stooges' day, with the average budget for feature films today running from $10 to $15 million and the cost of a one-minute commercial more than the cost of a dozen Stooges comedies. Harry Cohn would have been driven up the walls by the current budgets of feature films, especially when you realize that this was a man who used to run around the studio turning out the lights. But Harry would have gotten a kick out of the fact that, out of all of his classic, vintage films, it was the Three Stooges' 190 comedies that were still reaping in the millions a half-century later.

The powers that be at the present-day Columbia Pictures certainly owe Harry Cohn and the Three Stooges a debt of gratitude.

Director Del Lord and comedienne Joan Davis pose for the camera on the set of Kansas City Kitty *(1948).*

The Stars

Moe Howard

June 19, 1897-May 4, 1975

Moe Howard, the Stooges' leader, was born in Brooklyn, New York. He was the next to the youngest of Solomon and Jennie Horwitz's five sons. His education included grade school and the first two months of high school. He was thrown out of both of them. The acting bug had bit him and instead of studying, he would play court jester to his classmates and drive his teachers up the wall. His report card reflected his atrocious behavior, but his grades for achievement were always excellent.

As a youngster in high school, Moe appeared in a school production of "The Story of Nathan Hale," which he also directed.

Fascinated by the theater, he played hooky to watch the melodramas at many of the local playhouses. In 1914, at the age of seventeen, Moe had the chance to act in these plays for two summers aboard a Mississippi showboat, playing parts that ran the gamut from pimple-faced juveniles to wrinkled old crones.

Through 1919 and the early 1920's, Moe performed with the Marguerite Bryant Players, a stock company where he and his brother Shemp appeared in blackface. He followed this with one-night stands across the country as "Jimmy" in the play *Baby Mine,* and made a series of silent sports comedies with baseball great Honus Wagner.

Late in 1922, this stage-struck stooge with the Rose Bowl haircut joined his boyhood friend Ted Healy and, along with his brother Shemp, formed a show business partnership that would continue intermittently for almost a decade.

In 1925, blue-eyed Moe married brown-eyed Helen Schonberger, a cousin of the late Harry Houdini. They had two children: the author, who married producer, director and cartoonist Norman Maurer, and Paul, a freelance artist who lives in New York. Moe had three grandchildren: my two boys, Michael Maurer and Jeffrey Maurer Scott, and Paul's daughter Jennifer. (It is interesting to note that creativity runs in Moe's family, with grandson Jeffrey Scott a two-time Emmy Award winning writer on the Saturday morning television show, *Muppet Babies*, Michael Maurer a story-editor and writer on the prime-time television show *Facts of Life*, and Jennifer Howard a freshman in the school of animation at California Institute of the Arts).

In 1926, Helen urged Moe to leave show business. She was pregnant and, wanting her husband home for a change, convinced him to leave Healy for a career in the business world. It was a short-lived career that ended in a financial fiasco.

With Helen's blessings, Moe went back to

Healy and from 1929 to 1932 Healy, Moe and Shemp, in addition to vaudeville engagements, appeared in the J.J. Shubert production *A Night in Venice* and the Rube Goldberg feature film at Fox, *Soup to Nuts*. In 1932, when Shemp left the act to go to Vitaphone, Moe's younger brother Jerome "Curly" Howard took his place, joining Healy, Moe and Larry to make shorts and features at MGM.

It was in 1934 that Moe, Larry and Curly made the decision to leave Healy, and they signed a contract with Columbia Pictures to make the short *Woman Haters*.

This was followed by 189 two-reel comedies, filmed between 1934 and 1958. During this time, Moe would see two of his brothers die during their tenure in the Curly role, and, finally, after their Columbia contract was terminated, Curly's replacement, Joe Besser, would leave the act due to his wife's ill-health and Besser's inability to leave her to make personal appearances.

In 1958, our Stooge leader, determined to keep the act going, brought in his final Curly replacement, Joe DeRita, a pudgy comedian from burlesque who was promptly nicknamed "Curly-Joe."

At a Bakersfield nightclub, trying out their new act, the Stooges received a cool reception. Moe felt that this was finally the end of the Three Stooges as an act, but 1958 would prove to be just a turning point in their long career. Within the year, Columbia Pictures released 78 of their comedies to television and, overnight, the Three Stooges became the most popular children's show in the country.

The Stooges were on top again with appearances on the television shows of Danny Thomas, Ed Sullivan, Eddie Cantor, Steve Allen, Ed Wynn and Milton Berle. There were contracts by the hundreds for personal appearances, records and merchandising. In the space of six years, the Stooges made eight theatrical features, most of which were financially successful. The sixties were the Stooges' "golden years," but by 1969 the bubble had burst. The baby-boom audience that made them TV favorites was growing up and the television markets started to wane, along with the Stooges' popularity.

To keep the act in the public eye, Moe and his partners pooled their own money to produce a television pilot titled *Kook's Tour*, a comedy travelogue. It was during this production that Larry Fine had a major stroke. The film could not be completed without him and was promptly shelved.

Although this looked like the end of the act known as the Three Stooges, Moe, at seventy-three, refused to quit. He tried to make a solo comeback and appeared in several dramatic roles, continued to make television appearances on the *Mike Douglas Show* and toured the college lecture circuit, where he screened several two-reel comedies, spoke about them, answered questions and single-handedly recreated the Stooges' stage routine, taking on the roles of both Curly and Larry as well as his own.

Moe continued to perform until 1974 when he developed lung cancer and died the following year at the age of seventy-seven.

Larry Fine

October 5, 1902-January 4, 1975

Larry Fine, the Stooge with the frizzy mop top, was born Louis Feinberg, the son of Fanny Lieberman and jeweler Joseph Feinberg.

Larry attended South Walk Grammar School and Central High School in Philadelphia. During this period he joined his father's jewelry business but after three months was given a $100 bonus and two weeks salary to quit because he kept all the employees laughing and no work was getting done. His first professional job, at age fifteen, was singing along with movie slides at Philadelphia movie houses where he received $2 a performance.

During his school years, Larry was a violinist and conducted the school orchestra, finally quitting school to join Gus Edward's Newsboy Sextette, where he played his violin while dancing and telling jokes in a Jewish dialect. On the bill with him at the time was a pretty, petite blonde, Mabel Haney, who later would become his wife. Mabel and her sister joined Larry in an act called "The Haney Sisters and Fine." The three worked together in the United States and Canada until Larry was chosen by Ted Healy to become a Stooge, first appearing with Healy and Shemp in the J.J. Shubert show *A Night in Spain*. In 1929, Larry and Shemp were joined by Moe, who was back in show business again, and the three worked with Ted Healy in the Shubert show *A Night in Venice*. The remainder of Larry's career would parallel Moe's as poor Porcupine was pummeled and poked right up to and into his seventies.

Larry and Mabel had two children: a son, Johnny, and a daughter, Phyllis. Johnny died in a tragic automobile accident on November 17, 1961, at age 24, leaving a wife and three children. Phyllis married television actor and disc jockey Don Lamond. They have two children, Kris and Eric.

On January 4, 1975, Larry died of a stroke at the Motion Picture Country House. He will long be remembered for his ability to take everything that Moe had to dish out and be very funny in the process.

Jerome "Curly" Howard

October 22, 1903-January 18, 1952

Jerome Lester Horwitz, the shaven-headed Stooge was the youngest son of Jennie and Solomon Horwitz and was nicknamed "Babe" by his older brothers.

Curly has been described in previous books as a quiet, well-behaved, fair student who excelled in sports. I'm afraid I will have to amend the words quiet and well-behaved, as new research, gleaned from several interviews for his biography, tells me otherwise. I recently found out that he was far from quiet and chased the ladies at the early age of fifteen.

As a young man in his teens, Curly had two loves—music and girls. He was an accomplished ballroom dancer and loved to sing songs while he played his ukelele.

Sometime between 1928 and 1929, Curly had his first show-business experience, appearing on stage as a comedy musical conductor for Orville Knapp's Band. I recently learned that Curly married for the first time at age 26—bride unknown. It was a short-lived, hush-hush affair which was quickly nixed by his mother Jennie.

Curly's interest in the entertainment field grew as he watched his brothers Shemp and Moe perform with Ted Healy. When Shemp left the Stooges in 1932, Curly got his first big break when he was asked to take his place. Curly followed Healy's command to shave his head and his moustache and went on stage looking like a rotund little kid.

After the Stooges left Ted Healy, Curly starred in 97 of the 190 Three Stooges comedies. Curly was unquestionably a comedic genius whose unique characterization and myriad one-of-a-kind facial expressions ran the gamut and included bits of pantomime and crazy catch-phrases which were to become legend. It was Curly's unique talents which led to the team's rapid rise to success at Columbia . . . a success which also led to Curly's downfall. He ate too much, drank too much and made too much merry. Curly lived life to the hilt and bought dogs, houses and cars at a frenzied pace. It was almost as though he knew he hadn't much time.

Among the women he loved was his second

wife, Elaine Ackerman, whom he married on June 7, 1939. One year later his first child, Marilyn, was born and in 1940 this marriage also ended in divorce.

As Curly continued his bad habits and frenzied pace, his health began to decline and his blood pressure soared. In spite of this, he married his third wife, Marion Buxbaum, on October 17, 1945. The choice was disastrous and the two separated three months later and were divorced within the year. The stormy marriage to Marion and the messy court battle that ensued contributed to the deterioration of his health. On May 6, 1946, he suffered a stroke during the filming of his 97th comedy, *Half-Wits' Holiday*.

By 1947, Curly's condition had improved enough for him to marry his fourth wife, Valerie Newman, on July 30, 1947, and within the year, Valerie gave birth to a girl, Curly's second child, Janie.

The ensuing five years were spent in and out of hospitals, and on January 18, 1952, Curly died at Baldy View Sanitarium in the San Gabriel Valley at the age of forty-eight. The end of Curly's life could be viewed as being cut off in its prime, but anyone who thirty-four years after his death is able to continue bringing laughter to generation after generation of people must have done something right.

The Cast and Crew

FELIX ADLER—(Writer) *Restless Knights*

Felix Adler was born in 1891, and since he was rather a recluse, uncovering information on his early life was a next to impossible task.

Adler started in vaudeville as a singer and dancer before joining Mack Sennett at Keystone Studios in the 1920's, where he wrote catchy titles for silent movies and moved on to become a gag man.

At Keystone, Adler soon became head story writer, which included editing scripts and interviewing neophytes to the writing game. One such young, aspiring writer was Frank Capra, who described Adler as a "brash extrovert to whom life was just a bowl of gags."

During Adler's Keystone Comedy days he found himself involved in story conferences which, according to Mack Sennett, consisted of six gag men, Vernon Smith and himself. There was no order to this chaos. They would descend upon a story idea from every direction and anyone with a humorous bit would toss it in. One funny routine would bring to mind dozens of others, and often two gag men would combine their ideas into one routine. Writers would often act out their gags, and that is where the fun began.

Felix Adler, writer.

For example, one time Frank Capra had a scene with plumbers and actually crawled under his own sink to trigger ideas. Another time Felix Adler came to a conference equipped with milk and a rubber glove to demonstrate one of his ideas—a scene about a near-sighted farmer who milked a rubber glove instead of a cow.

Ed Bernds, who spent a lot of time with Adler in his Columbia days, could only recall that Adler lived alone up in the hills on Beachwood Drive, the famous street which used to bisect the Columbia lot. Beachwood Drive is now closed off and deadends at what was Columbia's old studio. It brought back pleasant memories when my son, Michael Maurer (who is currently story-editor and writer for the TV series *Facts of Life*), invited me to a taping of one of his shows and I found myself once again on that familiar old street, remembering those happy childhood days when I visited the set to watch Moe, Larry and Curly do their insane stuff.

After leaving Keystone, Adler moved to Columbia as a gag writer. During his long career

in comedy, he wrote for such stars as Will Rogers, Harold Lloyd, Laurel and Hardy, Abbott and Costello, as well as The Three Stooges.

On March 26, 1963, at the age of 72, Felix Adler died of cancer at the Motion Picture Country House.

LUCIEN BALLARD—(Director of Photography) *Yes, We Have No Bonanza*

Lucien Ballard was born on May 6, 1908, in Miami, Oklahoma. All that I was able to find out about his family background is that he was part Cherokee Indian. He spent time during his college years at both the University of Oklahoma and the University of Pennsylvania, graduating from neither school and winding up in China.

Upon returning to the States, he worked in sawmills and out in the woods as a surveyor. One day, during a visit to a girlfriend, who happened to be a script girl at Paramount, Ballard helped a cameraman load some equipment and found himself in the movie business, earning about $20 a week.

While at Paramount, he worked his way up the ladder, first as a cutter and assistant-cameraman and then assisting Lee Garmes on the 1930's film *Morocco*. It was during this period that he made a positive impression on director Joseph von Sternberg, who made him co-photographer on *The Devil Is a Woman* and director of photography on *Crime and Punishment*, both released in 1935.

Later, Ballard went to Columbia Pictures, where he filmed many forgettable B-movies. But it wasn't long after this that he distinguished himself as a master of black-and-white photography, and in later years his photographic talents expanded and he added excitement to many epic, outdoor Technicolor westerns. It seems ironic when one realizes that the acclaimed Lucien Ballard got his start in westerns working in 1939 on the Stooge's comedy *Yes, We Have No Bonanza*.

On June 26, 1945, Lucien Ballard married film star, Merle Oberon in a "proxy" ceremony at Juarez Mexico. Their marriage lasted until 1949. Ballard photographed many of Oberon's films. In fact, she insisted on having

Lucien Ballard, cinematographer.

him work on all her pictures and would not sign a contract unless he was put on as cameraman.

While at Fox, in the mid-fifties, Ballard was noted for photographing the beauties of that era. His career hit high gear at this point as he worked under such directors as Stanley Kubrick, Henry Hathaway and Sam Peckinpah.

Leonard Maltin, during an interview with Ballard for his book *The Art of the Cinematographer* asked him a question regarding the camera trickery used in the Stooges films. Ballard explained, "Everything was done on the set. If you wanted to show the Stooges driving a car into a garage, and then the car exploding, you'd put a trough filled with flash powder underneath the camera then set it off. You'd cut and your next shot would show the car with the fenders blown off, and the Stooges would be covered with black soot and appear to have been blown to various parts of the room."

Forty-seven years have passed since Lucien Ballard lensed his first Stooges comedy. He is now living in the California desert community of Indian Wells.

GEORGE BAXTER—(Actor) *Restless Knights*

George Baxter was born in Paris, France, on April 8, 1905. He spent his early years acting in radio and later made numerous films which included *Dinner at Eight, Lady and the Bandit, Island in the Sky, Lili, The Purple Gang* and *Lady in the Cage*. In the forties, he appeared with Helen Hayes on the New York stage, where he racked up many credits, including, *George Washington Slept Here, The Flag Is Born, Rebecca, Early to Bed* and *Green Hat*, which took him to Australia on tour with Judith Anderson.

Baxter's television credits include *Playhouse 90* and *One Man's Family* as well as numerous television commercials. His claim to fame in Stooges comedies was the film *Restless Knights*, in which he played the part of Count Boris.

George Baxter died on September 9, 1976, in New York. He is survived by a son and daughter.

George Baxter, actor.

WILLIAM S. BLYSTONE—(Actor) *Restless Knights*

William Stanley Blystone was born in Wisconsin on August 1, 1894. During his acting career he worked in both television and films, but the credit that we are most interested in was his role as Captain of the Guards in *Restless Knights*. It is interesting to note that Blystone was surrounded by people in the profession. His brother, Jack Blystone, was a director, and his wife, Alma Tell, whom he married in 1932, was an actress.

On July 16, 1956, at age 61, Blystone collapsed on a Hollywood street corner (Cahuenga and Waring) and was pronounced dead on arrival at Hollywood Receiving Hospital. At the time of his death he was still a member of the acting profession, having won a role in the Wyatt Earp TV series.

William S. Blystone, actor.

WALTER BRENNAN—(Actor) *Restless Knights*

For almost sixty years, gravel-voiced Walter Brennan brightened the screen in more films than even he was able to remember, including scores of silent films in which he appeared as an anonymous extra or a daredevil stunt man.

Walter Brennan, actor.

Brennan's list of film credits reached the hundreds, yet he originally planned to become an engineer.

Brennan, a descendant of New England pioneers, was born on July 25, 1894, at Swampscott, Massachusetts. His parents had every hope that their son would follow in his father's engineering footsteps. Walter began his secondary education at Rindge Technical School, Cambridge, planning to enroll eventually at Massachusetts Institute of Technology. However, the acting bug hit him in high school dramatics, and he changed his plans.

After two years of military service in Europe, Brennan returned to work for a time as a reporter for a Boston newspaper. Then, after marrying his childhood sweetheart, Ruth Wells, he moved to Southern California.

Brennan, and a then unknown Montana cowboy, Gary Cooper, haunted studio casting offices without much success. (They remained good friends for years, appearing together in many films.) After months of work as an extra, Brennan made his stunt man debut in the 1923 thriller *Lorraine of the Lions*, in which one of his stunts was driving a car off the end of a pier into the Pacific Ocean at 50 mph. Brennan joked at the time, "There was another dummy in the car with me, but he had his hat nailed on!"

A decisive impact was made on his career when, in an accident in 1932, many of his teeth were knocked out. A set of false teeth enabled him to remove or restore his dentures from part to part, depending on the age of the character he was portraying.

In 1934, Brennan played a supporting role (a train conductor) in *Woman Haters*, the first Columbia Three Stooges comedy, starring Larry, Moe and Curly. According to Moe, Brennan came into the Stooges' dressing room after the completion of the comedy, apologized for giving such a poor performance and told Moe that he was giving up acting and returning to Massachusetts. Moe claimed he talked Brennan into giving acting another shot, and Brennan, convinced, remained in Hollywood. Shortly thereafter he appeared in *Restless Knights*.

Brennan's big break came in 1935, when

Samuel Goldwyn signed him for *Wedding Night*. His performance won him a long-term contract with MGM and the Academy Award winning role in *Come and Get It*. He repeated again as an Oscar winner with *Kentucky* (1938) and *The Westerner* (1940).

Brennan also appeared in such memorable films as *Pride of the Yankees, Sergeant York, Meet John Doe, My Darling Clementine, Red River* and *Bad Day at Black Rock*. Later in his career, he made two popular television series, *The Real McCoys* and *The Tycoon*.

In 1967, Brennan appeared in my husband Norman's feature *Who's Minding the Mint?* at Columbia, where he celebrated his seventy-fifth birthday on the set and Moe came down to visit. It was a grand reunion after over thirty years and Brennan, upon seeing my father, immediately started to reminisce about his poor performance in *Woman Haters* and thanked Moe profusely for talking him into continuing with his acting career.

In his autumn years, Brennan and his wife lived on a 10-acre grapefruit ranch in the rural community of Moorpark about 60 miles and 60 minutes by freeway from Hollywood. Brennan had three children: Walter, Arthur and Ruth.

Walter Brennan died on September 22, 1974, in Oxnard, California, after a long battle with emphysema.

Dick Curtis, actor. ▲   ▼ *Vernon Dent, actor.*

DICK CURTIS—(Actor) *We Want Our Mummy*

Steely-eyed Dick Curtis played "Mr. Mean" in hundreds of B-Westerns and was frequently seen making his evil eyes in serials including *Mandrake the Magician* and *Terry and the Pirates*. Some of his more important features were *King Kong, Jack London* and *My Six Convicts*. In 1939, Curtis appeared in the Stooges comedy, *Yes, We Have No Bonanza*, in the role of Mr. Mean again. Dick Curtis died in 1952, the same year as Curly Howard.

VERNON DENT—(Actor) *Yes, We Have No Bonanza*

Vernon Dent was born in 1895. He started his career as a film comedian and appeared in Mack Sennett, Mermaid and Educational comedies before getting his break in features. In the thirties, he turned to screen writing, but continued with his acting career.

Sometime in the early thirties, Dent joined the Columbia Pictures stock company of supporting players and appeared in a multitude of Stooges comedies, almost always playing the part of the heavy.

Humorous as it sounds, Dent's getting married hinged on whether Harry Langdon, motion picture comedian, and his wife stayed married for five years. When Dent proposed to Miss Eunice Borroughs in 1933, she shook her head and declared: "Hollywood marriages are jinxed. But if the Langdons are still married five years from now I might change my mind." The Langdons stayed together and Vernon and Eunice were married in 1938. The following year he played the part of the sheriff in the Stooges comedy, *Yes, We Have No Bonanza*.

Vernon Dent died on November 5, 1963, at the age of 68.

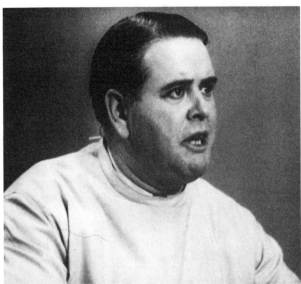

Bud Jamison, actor.

BUD JAMISON—(Actor) *We Want Our Mummy*

Bud Jamison had a long, long career in films, dating back to the days of Harold Lloyd and Charlie Chaplin.

Jamison was born in Vallejo, California, in 1894. He acted not only on Hollywood's silver screen but appeared on the legitimate stage and in vaudeville as well. Just a few of his film roles with the cream of Hollywood's comics were: *Wrong Doctor,* with Edgar Kennedy; *The Dentist,* starring W.C. Fields; *It Always Happens,* starring Andy Clyde; and *Nothing But Pleasure* and *General Nuisance*, both Buster Keaton comedies. Jamison appeared in a variety of parts in Three Stooges comedies, including his role as Professor Wilson in *We Want Our Mummy*.

This very prolific and versatile actor certainly left his mark in the history of two-reelers. He died on September 10, 1944, in Hollywood.

BENJAMIN KLINE—(Photographer) *Restless Knights*

Benjamin Kline was born on July 11, 1897, in Alabama, where his father, a department store owner in Birmingham, had immigrated from Germany and married his mother, a second-generation Alabaman.

Kline first worked in New York as a cameraman and moved to California when he was in his early twenties.

At Universal Studios, he met and married cashier Annette Halprin, whose father, Sol Halprin, was head of both the camera department and the film lab at 20th Century-Fox. The two had five children: three girls, Barbara, Harriet and Vicki, and two boys, Richard and Henry, both of whom entered the film business, Richard as a cinematographer and Henry as a production manager.

In his early days at Columbia, Kline worked on many of the Three Stooges comedies, including *Restless Knights*. Kline's television credits included *The Fireside Theatre, Wagon Train* and the *Virginian*. He was active in television until the seventies and died in 1974 at the age of 75.

Benjamin Kline, cinematographer. ▼

SEARLE KRAMER—(Writer) *We Want Our Mummy* and *Yes, We Have No Bonanza*

Searle Kramer was born to Charles and Lena Kramer on April 6, 1910. His parents came over from Europe, finally settling in Chicago, Illinois. Searle and his brother Bert lived in the Illinois area until they moved to Jackson, Michigan, where Searle graduated from Jackson High.

In 1935, at the young age of twenty-five,

Searle was hired by producer-director Jules White to write the Stooges short *We Want Our Mummy*.

When I asked Searle what he thought of his assignment with the Stooges, he chuckled and said, "I loved it." His collaboration with Elwood Ullman produced five Three Stooges comedies.

In 1942 Kramer was drafted into the Army and was assigned to the Signal Corps' Photo Center in New York City where, until the end of the war, he wrote the top-secret "Staff Reports." During this period he also wrote two plays and two motion pictures.

Kramer's credits also include *A Missing Fortune* and *Quizz Whiz*. In the sixties he moved over to television, writing segments of *The Flying Nun* and *I Dream of Jeannie*. The high point in Kramer's career—as sheer enjoyment—was the film *Mr. Universe*.

Searle Kramer retired in 1978. He currently resides in Beverly Hills with his wife Jan.

CHARLES LAMONT—(Director)
Restless Knights

Charles Lamont was born on May 5, 1895, in San Francisco, California. A fourth generation

Charles Lamont, director.

performer, he appeared on stage in his teens and in films starting in 1919.

In 1922, Lamont turned director, starting with comedy shorts which he made for Sennett, Christie and others. He began his directorial work in features in the mid-1930's, taking the helm of a number of comedies at Universal Studios, including the "Ma and Pa Kettle" films and those of Abbott and Costello. In 1935, Lamont directed two-reelers with the Three Stooges. His first experience with these three zany comedians was the film *Restless Knights*. During an interview, Lamont was quoted as saying, "I made them [the Stooges] follow the script. If there was anything I didn't like, I'd cut it out. I was never a great admirer of ad-libs."

It is interesting to note that several of Lamont's Westerns and exotic-adventure films acquired a cult following. Several French critics spoke highly of his two 1945 films with Yvonne De Carlo and Rod Cameron, *Salome, Where She Danced*, and *Frontier Gal*.

I wrote to Charles Lamont in March of 1986, and he was kind enough to telephone me. When I questioned him regarding his thoughts on the Stooges, he explained, "Curly was quiet most of the time but it depended on the mood he was in. Moe was the boss of the act and Larry didn't contribute a great deal to what was going on." When he made this remark about Larry, I laughed and related my experience of the week before.

As I was going through the frames of *Restless Knights*, making my selections, I came across a sequence in which Moe and Curly were going through a very difficult wrestling routine and there in the background was Larry, seated in a chair where he appeared to be fast asleep. I was dying to find out if this was part of the script, but Mr. Lamont could not recall—and reminded me that this film was made over fifty years ago.

Charles Lamont is presently living in the Lodge at the Motion Picture Country House in Calabasas. His wife, Estelle, was with him the day I spoke to him and was kind enough to trust me with the wonderful, old family photograph of her husband taken in the thirties, which was used to illustrate this biography.

Ted Lorch, actor.

Del Lord, director.

TED LORCH—(Actor) *Yes, We Have No Bonanza*

Ted Lorch was born in 1873 in Springfield, Illinois, and died November 12, 1947, in Hollywood. He was an actor of screen, stage and radio. His face was seen in many of the Three Stooges comedies, several of which were: *Goofs and Saddles, Uncivil Warbirds, Hot Scots, Half-Wits' Holiday* (Curly's last comedy) and *We Want Our Mummy*, in the role of the kidnapper.

DEL LORD—(Director) *Yes, We Have No Bonanza* and *We Want Our Mummy*

Del Lord, according to Mack Sennett, was an "Ace comedy director." And in the area of short comedies he was probably without peer.

Lord had a long and distinguished career during the silent era. He had no pretenses about his work—it was just slapstick comedy—but one must admit he did it well. His shorts were his best work. His features, some of which were *Blonde from Brooklyn, Trapped by Television* and *I Love a Bandleader*, were entertaining, but the hundreds of shorts to his credit were where he excelled.

Lord was born in Grimsley, Canada, in 1894 and went to California with a friend, William Collier. After appearing in numerous Keystone Comedies, he went over to Fox, and from 1927

to 1928 he worked for First National and United Artists; then came a stint for Educational Pictures and Mack Sennett, and in 1930 he was directing the Vitaphone Varieties for Universal.

According to Leonard Maltin, in his book *The Great Movie Shorts*, Jules White found Del Lord selling used cars, realized that he was once one of Mack Sennett's greatest directors, and hired him immediately to direct shorts at Columbia.

Maltin quoted actress Ann Doran when she reminisced about her days at Columbia Pictures: "Without a doubt, he [Lord] was the most even-tempered man I have ever known. He never tired, he was inventive. His sense of humor and timing was infallible. Charley [Chase] and Del had the same marvelous feeling for timing that Jack Benny has. It is an inborn sense."

In 1935 Del Lord first directed the Stooges in the short *Pop Goes the Easel*. He followed this by directing the next four Stooges comedies, and then in 1939 he was at the helm of both *We Want Our Mummy* and *Yes, We Have No Bonanza*.

According to Sennett, Del Lord was a champion pie thrower as well as fine stunt man and racing car driver. Even after he became a director, he drove the paddy wagon in the Keystone Cops' chase sequences.

As a director, he was famous for shooting his pictures backwards; first he would photograph the climax of a film, then start at the beginning and work up to his ending.

Del Lord died on March 23, 1970. He was retired at the time and living in Vista, California, with his wife Edith. He would have found it ironic that the work that he would be best remembered for would be those classic comedies with the Three Stooges.

WILLIAM LYON—(Editor)
Restless Knights

Among the most unsung of off-screen technicians is the film editor who has the capacity of coming up with a super creation or literally destroying a film. The editor, working closely with the director, has the job of cutting down the miles of film exposed during shooting.

William Lyon, one of the most eminent film editors, was a two-time Academy Award winner for his work on *From Here to Eternity* and *Picnic,* and three-time nominee for *The Jolson Story, The Caine Mutiny* and *Cowboy.*

Lyon was born in Dennison, Texas, but was raised in Los Angeles where he moved when he was 12 and went to work at age 14. He had jobs with Pacific Electric, electrical supply firms and other fields far removed from films, but became interested in editing when sound came in. He was introduced to the industry by friends, and spent most of his career at Columbia Pictures.

Looking back on his Columbia days, Lyon said about Harry Cohn, the head of Columbia Studios, "He was the greatest showman in the industry. He ran the studio singlehandedly. He made many enemies and could be very hard-handed and crude, but I, personally, can't say enough good about him." Moe Howard had similar words to say about Cohn.

Lyon started as first-assistant film editor at the old Fox Western Avenue lot in 1927. As an assistant film editor at Columbia in 1930, he worked on Harry Langdon and Andy Clyde shorts and later on countless Westerns where he learned the fundamentals of timing and became a full-fledged editor in 1935, working on the Stooges comedy *Restless Knights* in that same year.

At Columbia, Lyon was an assistant-editor on many of Frank Capra's famed pictures. He entered the Army in September, 1941, and even before Pearl Harbor, was hard at work editing Army films for the Capra motion picture unit.

After the war, Lyon was discharged from the Army on October 15, 1945, with the rank of captain. Within the week he was back at Columbia editing *The Jolson Story.*

William Lyon died March 19, 1974.

EDDIE LAUGHTON—(Actor) *We Want Our Mummy*

Eddie Laughton, who began his career as a soprano in a boy's church choir, was described by one biographer as "a screen villain of the deepest dye."

Laughton's full name was Edgar Hugh Laughton. He was born in Sheffield, England, on June 20, 1902. He came over to the United States at an early age and was educated at Hudson School for Boys in New York and Detroit Grammar and High School.

Laughton made his acting debut at the Jesse Bonstelle Stock Company, where his sister was stage manager. He later became a master of ceremonies and leader of a dance orchestra

Eddie Laughton, actor.

49

with which he appeared in theatres and night clubs from coast to coast. These engagements brought him into contact with the Three Stooges, who were in need of a "straight man." Looking for someone with whom to contrast their mad, slapstick antics, the trio persuaded Laughton to join them.

When Columbia engaged the Stooges for their series of two-reel comedies, Moe recommended Laughton to the head of the Short Subjects Department. In the years that followed, Laughton played roles in many of the Stooges shorts, including that of the taxi driver in *We Want Our Mummy*.

Some time later, he left the Stooges to do dramatic roles at Columbia and worked with them only on personal appearance tours, including their tour of England and its provinces in 1939. In 1939 he also appeared with them in *George White's Scandals*, at the Manhattan Night Club and at the Casa Mañana.

A few of Laughton's feature credits at Columbia were: *Smashing the Spy Ring, Texas Stagecoach, Highway Patrol* and *The Doctor Takes a Wife*.

Eddie Laughton died on February 21, 1952, at the age of fifty, one month after Curly Howard.

GENEVA MITCHELL—(Actress)
Restless Knights

Geneva Mitchell was born on March 3, 1907, in McClarysville, Indiana. She acted on both screen and stage, appearing in the Stooges shorts *Hoi Polloi* and *In the Sweet Pie and Pie*, which was a remake of *Hoi Polloi*. Several of her feature film appearances were: *World Gone Mad, Morning Glory,* and *Air Hawks*. Geneva Mitchell played the part of the beautiful queen in *Restless Knights*.

CHARLES NELSON—(Editor) *Yes, We Have No Bonanza*

While doing research at the Margaret Herrick Library at the Academy of Motion Picture Arts and Sciences, the only biographical data I could find on Charles Nelson is as follows: a short article in a newsletter put out by the Park

Geneva Mitchell, actress.

LaBrea Apartments in which they mentioned that Charles Nelson was nominated four times for an Oscar but won only one Academy Award, for the film *Picnic*.

Not wanting to have a blank in the biography section of the book, I wrote to Mr. Nelson and asked him if he would be willing to answer some questions about his film career. It seems that Mr. Nelson's privacy means a great deal to him, and he refused to be interviewed.

Elwood Ullman, screenwriter.

ELWOOD ULLMAN—(Writer) *We Want Our Mummy* and *Yes, We Have No Bonanza*

Elwood Ullman came to Hollywood in the late 1920's after working as a journalist in St. Louis. He worked primarily for Columbia Pictures and RKO Studios on the comedy two-reelers popular in the thirties and forties, and also worked at Universal and Monogram. Of the 190 Three Stooges films, Ullman was credited with writing nearly 100 of them.

Elwood wrote the screenplays for many comedy features, which included films for Bud Abbott and Lou Costello, Dean Martin and Jerry Lewis, the "Bowery Boys" and "Ma and Pa Kettle."

In the sixties, Ullman wrote the screenplay for *Snow White and the Three Stooges* and followed that a short time later with the Stooges' Columbia features, which included *The Three Stooges Meet Hercules, The Three Stooges in Orbit, The Three Stooges Go Around the World in a Daze* and *The Outlaws Is Coming*. Later on in his career, he wrote the dramatic screenplay *Battle Flame* and then the musical *Tickle Me*, starring Elvis Presley.

Ullman contributed many short stories to *The Saturday Evening Post* as well as articles for *Esquire* and *Country Gentleman* and travel pieces for several newspapers. His brother Furth, his only remaining relative, was recently interviewed after Ullman's death on October 11, 1985, and said Elwood was 82 when he died at his Hollywood home of an apparent heart attack.

JULES WHITE—(Associate Producer) *We Want Our Mummy* and *Yes, We Have No Bonanza*

Jules White was born in Budapest, Hungary, on September 17, 1900. He was one of four brothers, all of whom had successful careers in the film business: director Sam White, cameraman Ben White, and producer Jack White, who also wrote under the pseudonym of Preston Black and was one of the early creators and innovators of film comedy.

In 1910, White began his career with Pathe Films as a juvenile actor. Fortunately, his fam-

ily had settled in Edendale, a Los Angeles suburb which was the first home of most of the movie companies when they moved to the West Coast.

During his career as a child actor, White appeared in several movie milestones, playing an extra in *The Birth of a Nation* and the 1914 version of *The Spoilers*. He progressed rapidly from extra to bit-player, helped along by an Indian director, James Youngdeer. Youngdeer was taken with this precocious nine-year-old who would sing to him on the drive to and from location. White would serenade Youngdeer for the grand sum of fifty cents. If he worked in the film, he'd earn an extra fifty cents.

By 1920, White had gained experience in every phase of the movie business and that year found him at Educational Studios, working as an editor on his brother Jack White's comedies. Five years later, he was directing, and for the next half-decade he alternated between Educational and Fox Films.

White's career was certainly varied. At MGM he directed sports shorts; later on, "The Barkies," which were his favorite (an assortment of shorts starring dogs dressed up as

Jules White, director.

nally, as co-director, he worked with Zion Myers on the feature *Sidewalks of New York*, starring Buster Keaton.

Throughout his Columbia years, White, as head of the Short Subjects Department, produced and directed hundreds of films, which included classic comedies from veteran comedians such as Vera Vague, Buster Keaton, Charlie Chase, Harry Langdon, Hugh Herbert, Leon Errol, Tom Kennedy and Andy Clyde. If White did nothing else, that would have been a fine tribute to the man, but he went on to direct and produce the bulk of the Three Stooges' 190 two-reel comedies and remained as head of Columbia's Short Subjects Department until 1959.

In 1960 he directed the Columbia feature *Stop! Look! and Laugh!* which was a compilation of Three Stooges shorts and shortly thereafter was co-creator of the CBS television series *Oh, Those Bells!*

A founding member of the Directors Guild of America, he served for many years on the Guild's board. He was also a member of the Board of Governors for the Academy of Motion Picture Arts and Sciences from 1945–1947.

During the early 1980's, White lived with his wife Judith in the San Fernando Valley. It was during this period that he was honored by the Academy of Motion Picture Arts and Sciences for his very meaningful contribution to the film industry.

On April 30, 1985, Jules White died of Alzheimer's disease. He is survived by his widow Judith, brother Sam White, son Richard, sister Ruth Brand, brother-in-law Judge Edward Brand and seven grandchildren.

1935
The Year of
RESTLESS KNIGHTS

On stage during a promotional tour with an audience of enthralled young fans.

The nation in 1935 was down in the dumps and Hollywood was there to provide an escape. Some 85 million people a week went to their local theatres, paying 25 cents a ticket (10 cents for kids). There were double, sometimes triple, features and give-aways at the door which included free hairdos, raffle tickets for shiny new automobiles and even photographs of the Three Stooges.

Audiences flocked to see such motion picture classics as *Naughty Marietta*, *Top Hat* and *David Copperfield*, and most of them were clean, escapist films. Producers had no other choice, as Hollywood, during the thirties, had a long list of taboos: long kisses, adultery, double beds, words like "hell" and "damn"—even babies in films had to wear their diapers. Despite these strict censorship codes, the Three Stooges' slapstick went unnoticed as

they banged and bopped each other in seven films. Obviously, there was no taboo on violence.

Although President Roosevelt said, "I see one-third of the nation ill-housed, ill-clad, ill-nourished," the Stooges and especially Curly were certainly well nourished as they were in the lucky two-thirds and were paid adequately for their slapstick comedy. Larry, Moe and Curly were no longer earning the pittance that Ted Healy had doled out to them at MGM the year before. Now the three were making $1,000 a week split three ways—which for the Depression era was pretty good money.

According to sound man Lodge Cunningham, an incident occurred regarding that $1,000 salary which could certainly have made a Stooges comedy in itself. Lodge chuckled as he told me that each week, like clockwork, the

Larry Fine with daughter Phyllis (1930's).

Larry and Moe—on and off screen they're still Stooges.

54

Proud father Moe and serious son Paul.

Stooges would go to the local bank to cash their pay check. Moe, the spokesman, would always carry the check, with Larry and Curly close at his heels. The bank teller was always braced for the event, having the exact amount of cash on hand—$1,000 divided into three, neat bundles with three hundred and thirty-three dollars and thirty-three cents in each. The comedy began as the Stooges went through a silly routine to see who would get the odd cent, the fate of which would always be decided by Moe, Larry and Curly, huddled in a circle in the lobby of the bank, matching pennies.

A portent of the world upheaval that would come later on in the thirties was the sudden death of the Treaty of Versailles in March of 1935 when the German government, without warning, proclaimed the re-establishment of the German Army.

But America looked the other way and eased the burden of its problems during these Depression years by escaping to the local movie houses. The motion pictures nominated for Academy Awards in 1935 ran the gamut from serious films like *The Informer* and *Mutiny on the Bounty* to light bits of fluff like *Naughty Marietta* and *Broadway Melody*. The film *The Informer* won the Award for best picture. And

sometime in this same year the Academy's golden trophy was given the nickname "Oscar."

In the previous year, 1934, the Stooges were nominated for that little gold statuette for their film *Men in Black*—the same year that they made *Woman Haters, Punch Drunks* and *Three Little Pigskins.*

With millions of Americans out of work, the Stooges were glad, in these Depression days of 1935, to be making seven shorts that year at Columbia and even more delighted to be able to perform in vaudeville during their twelve-week layoff period. The seven shorts for Columbia released in 1935 were: *Horses' Collars, Restless Knights, Pop Goes the Easel, Uncivil Warriors, Pardon My Scotch, Three Little Beers* and *Hoi Polloi.*

When I recall the film *Hoi Polloi,* I always think of my mother who got into the Stooges' act in 1935 when she came up with the story line for that film. The idea was triggered by the famous George Bernard Shaw story *Pygmalion,* which had the same classic thread running through it as the play and film *My Fair Lady.* The story line concerned an argument as to whether it was environment or heredity that

The author with brother Paul, who refuses to smile for the camera.

55

Larry's daughter Phyllis, a bit wary about petting Curly's current dog.

produced a gentleman. One man insisted it was environment and bet that he could make a silk purse out of a sow's ear. What better idea, thought my mother, than to turn three sow's ears into three silk purses, and so in *Hoi Polloi* the Three Stooges, playing garbage collectors, would become "gentlemen." Poor Helen was paid for her idea in Depression wages. She had the choice of a film credit or $50 and took the latter.

Like my mother, I also had a shot at show business during 1935. I appeared in a film that year which broke no records, but drew praise from the critics for its emotional tension. It starred Ann Harding, Herbert Marshall and Franchot Tone and was titled *The Flame Within*, which, I am proud to say, was the vehicle for my second acting role. My part was a "silent bit." All I had to do was stick my head through a doorway and make faces at Franchot Tone. According to the script, he was sup-

posed to stare at this strange-looking child and think he had a case of the D.T.'s. When the director saw my funny freckled face, the part was mine. And, need I say, my father was thrilled when everyone on the set cracked up at the sight of me. Because of this he was certain I was going to be a comedienne. How wrong he was. Even now, I can't tell a "knock-knock" joke without messing up the punchline.

My third motion-picture role—and the seventh comedy for the Stooges—*Pop Goes the Easel*, was the only time Larry's daughter Phyllis and I appeared together in a film. I was eight years old in 1935 and Phyllis was two years my junior. At this point in time I had two films under my belt and felt like a pro. I thought of Phyllis as a neophyte and, since there were no lines and no close-ups in our scene, I thought this film was going to be a breeze.

Such was not the case. That day, on the set

A smiling Helen with the the apple of Moe's eye, Paul.

of *Pop Goes the Easel*, I found myself having a severe case of nerves. This was the first time I had worked with my father and I was deathly afraid that I might upset him if I held up shooting for any reason. Even at the young age of eight, I was aware of the Stooges' limited shooting schedule. Phyllis on the other hand knew nothing of shooting schedules. She was quite shy and seemed bewildered by the events taking place around her. After director Del Lord explained what we were to do, I can recall playing big sister and taking her through her paces. In the film, if you look carefully you can see me take Phyllis by the hand and pull her up during the action.

That day comes to mind as though it were yesterday. The street on Columbia's ranch in the Valley looked like a typical, small-town city street—Anywhere, U.S.A. Phyllis and I were supposed to be two ordinary little girls playing hopscotch on the sidewalk in front of a

small house. The Stooges, as was usually the case, were being chased, this time by a policeman and another man. Without glancing in either direction and without pause, the Stooges raced into the shot, pushed Phyllis and me aside, hopped through the hopscotch game and continued to race down the street with the men in hot pursuit. Although this was a complicated shot, it went off in one take as though it had been choreographed and a flood of relief washed over me. Despite the fact that my part was a minor one, the fuss everyone made over me made me feel like a movie star who had just been given an Academy Award. And even more important than that, I had not interfered with my father's tight shooting schedule.

In later years, I recall that Phyllis had no interest in watching the shorts being made. Her first love had always been sitting in the first row of a theatre and watching the Stooges in the flesh as they clobbered each other on a

The author and cousin Morton Howard (Shemp's son) in front of 107 S. Fuller, Moe and Helen's current residence (1935).

Moe with the author's first dog, Buttons (1935).

vaudeville stage. She and her mother, Mabel, followed Larry on almost every Three Stooges personal appearance tour, which resulted in the Fine family leading a rather nomadic life in the early days as they moved from town to town and hotel to hotel.

Phyllis spent hours on end backstage with Larry, and to her this was the most exciting part of the Stooges' entire career. My family, on the other hand, usually remained at home in California. Occasionally, when it was summer vacation, my mother would pack our bags and we'd train to the east coast to stay with my father during his many tours of the eastern seaboard.

Now, as I look back, I must agree with Phyllis that the excitement of vaudeville had something that films would never have. The live audience and live music was indescribable and I often found myself enthralled, standing backstage and watching the Stooges perform. But, as much as I loved vaudeville and traveling by train, I loved staying home even more. I

hated to miss school and, although it made me nervous, in my own way I enjoyed my film work and the feeling of importance it gave me.

When I first started working in pictures, I was as shy as Phyllis. I was the type who hated to stand out in the crowd and usually kept secret the fact that my father was a Stooge and that I was an actress. I don't think Moe took into consideration that side of my personality or he never would have taken me to Republic studio when I was seven to try out for my first film role. He was so giving that I just couldn't disappoint him by saying no. In spite of myself, I got the part—in a film titled *I'll Fix It,* with two old-timers, Jack Holt and Winnie Lightner. I played the role of a bratty kid who

Helen, the author, Paul and Moe, fall of 1935. Little Paul takes his first train ride back to California.

was required to knock a bowlful of nuts out of her piano teacher's hand when they were offered to her, and then deliver the line, "Ah nuts." How's that for stardom?

During the year of *Restless Knights*, I recall living with my parents in a rented house in Los Angeles at 107 South Fuller. In June of that year, despite the fact that my mother was expecting a baby, we left for New York, as she wanted to be near my father. While Moe delivered his slapstick punishment in a Boston theatre, my mother would deliver her baby at the Doctors' Hospital in New York City.

On July 8th my brother was born and my father was ecstatic. He'd always wanted a son. Several days later, waiting to be picked up at

Paul Alan Howard

July 8th, 1935

Mr. and Mrs. Moe H. Howard

Paul's birth announcement, its engraving still intact but its traditional blue ribbon faded to white after fifty-one years.

A July 8th telegram from Helen's New York hospital to Moe's vaudeville theater in Boston. The "gutters" refer to Moe's threat of getting drunk if Helen has a boy.

THE COMPANY WILL APPRECIATE SUGGESTIONS FROM ITS PATRONS CONCERNI   ITS SERVICE

1201-S

CLASS OF SERVICE

This is a full-rate Telegram or Cablegram unless its deferred character is indicated by a suitable symbol above or preceding the address.

WESTERN UNION (57)

R. B. WHITE
PRESIDENT

NEWCOMB CARLTON
CHAIRMAN OF THE BOARD

J. C. WILLEVER
FIRST VICE-PRESIDENT

SYMBOLS

DL = Day Letter
SER = Serial
NM = Night Message
NL = Night Letter
CDE = Code Cable
LC = Deferred Cable
NLT = Cable Night Letter
Ship Radiogram

The filing time shown in the date line on telegrams and day letters is STANDARD TIME at point of origin.   Time of receipt is STANDARD TIME at point of destination.

Received at 203 Tremont Street. Boston. Mass.

BAM136 27=YV NEWYORK NY 8 1145A

5 JUL 8 AM 11 59

MINUTES IN TRANSIT

FULL-RATE   DAY LETTER

MOE HOWARD=

    METROPOLITAN THEATRE=

ITS A GORGEOUS 8 POUND BOY BORN NINE FORTY FIVE AM KEEP OUT

OF THE GUTTERS CALL DOCTORS HOSPITAL TONIGHT BEFORE NINE

ROOM TWELVE NAUGHT SIX LOVE=

    HELEN.

THE QUICKEST, SUREST AND SAFEST WAY TO SEND MONEY IS BY TELEGRAPH OR CABLE

The author and actress Winnie Lightner in the film
I'll Fix It.

the hospital by my father, my mother was shocked to see a disheveled Moe, sporting a black eye and several cuts on his face. "No," he told her, "this didn't happen on stage stoogeing around." As she learned later, Moe was in an accident on the way to the hospital. While driving through a heavy rainstorm in a rented car and trying to manuever about on New York's antiquated version of the freeway, the car skidded and smashed into a very tall cement lamppost, knocking it off its foundation. The post fell in the direction of the car, coming down with a thunderous crash across the hood, smashing the windshield. My aunt, who was pregnant at the time, was seated in the back seat of the car. An ambulance was called which rushed a bruised Moe into the hospital emergency room and my aunt into the delivery room where my cousin Carole was born two months prematurely.

After the accident, my father who had stopped smoking for the umpteenth time, started up again. I suppose he felt his life was charmed, coming out of the accident unscathed, and that smoking would never do him in. For years he had smoked cigarettes. This time he chose cigars.

During the Stooges' vaudeville tours, Moe had a tremendous amount of time on his hands and between performances one could usually find him backstage in his dressing room, smoking away. He was quite a sight to see and I still cringe whenever I recall my father's stage attire, which was always the same, a conglomeration of sweaty, bedraggled, ill-fitting formal wear. Poor, uptight Moe. He just couldn't relax. He had to be doing something every minute. If he wasn't on stage, he'd be backstage hooking a rug for my mother or puffing away endlessly on cigars. Smoking seemed to be the answer for him, a way to soothe the savage Stooge.

While Moe was residing permanently in California except for his vaudeville tours, Larry and his family were always on the go, spending winters in Florida, summers in Atlantic City and, while he was working on the Columbia shorts, residing at the Knickerbocker Hotel in Hollywood. His family was always with him and not until he purchased a home in the mid-forties did they finally settle down.

Recently, I came across a newspaper article about Larry by columnist Bob Lancaster which I felt painted a rather poignant picture of the man. Lancaster wrote, "In his heyday, Larry Fine the movie star lived in a kind of semi-anonymity. Everybody knew him as one of the Three Stooges. They knew him by the various insulting but not demeaning nicknames that Moe Howard was always pinning on him.

Nicknames that almost invariably had to do with his ungodly head of hair. Nicknames like Porcupine, which every kid in the world affectionately modified to Porkypine. The hair style was early Art Garfunkle, a kind of unkempt Caucasian Afro—bald in the middle, a fringe fright wig without the wig, a giant egg sticking out of a windblown Easter basket—and it was by this hair style that millions knew him." Lancaster went on to say, "Moe Howard told me he'd always thought Larry's role in the Stooge routines was the hardest. He was always the third man in the act, hemmed in on one side by the zany scheming leader of the pack and on the other by the numskull fall guy."

In 1935, the "fall guy" was dating fast and furiously but would not marry again until 1937. I recall being on the school playground one day when a rather sweet, shy-looking girl whom I had befriended told me that her mother was going out with Curly. I remember my shock—naive child that I was—when she explained that her mother was a "divorcee." The super-clean movies of the thirties had led me to believe that divorce was a fate worse than death. But then this carousing around with divorcees was to be expected, as Curly was the

The Stooges practicing their table manners for the film Hoi Polloi.

Larry and Mabel Fine's residence during 1935, the Knickerbocker Hotel in Hollywood.

61

METRO

EDW. G. ROBINSON IN THE LAST GA

METRO SWEET SHOP   70¢ Good AMERICAN FEATURE

A theater somewhere in U.S.A. in the mid-thirties.

Sometime in the mid-thirties the Three Stooges made their first merchandising tie-in with the Pillsbury Farina Company, a manufacturer of breakfast cereals. Along with photographs, they gave away a cardboard Motion Picture Machine at local theatres across the country. The promo copy describes the Machine as, "A clever Moving Picture Machine in which you can actually see the Three Stooges in action." The ad continued, "Just turn the crank and watch your favorite comedy stars in action."

The Stooges posing with their give-away photos.

Giveaway photo from the 1930's.

Three frames from Three Little Pigskins *used in Pillsbury Motion Picture Machine.*

63

I wish I could recall the name of the famous prizefighter that Curly, Moe and Larry are in awe of.

Horses Collars, *1935*.

64

black sheep of the family, and I recall the hushed tones that my parents sometimes used when they talked about him.

Time and time again my father tried to guide his chubby, will-o'-the-wisp brother onto a more conventional path. But Curly was never bothered by my father's disapproval. He knew that his brother loved him no matter what he did and, despite my father's attempts to get him to settle down, he continued to feed his desires, which included sizable doses of wine, women and song.

Song was big in 1935 and something that Curly reveled in. The big band had become big business and in the thirties the band leader was a celebrity. Curly and the Stooges played on the same bill with almost all of them—Benny Goodman, Artie Shaw, the Dorseys, to name but a few. This was the era of "swing" and Curly's favorite sport was going to the late night spots where he would rip the table cloths or clack the back of two teaspoons together to the beat of the music. If he had consumed enough liquor, he'd have the courage to jump on the bandstand, grab the bass drum away from any musician that would let him have it and play like a madman. He was extremely good and both the band and the audience loved his antics.

And so, as 1935 wreaked havoc on the nation, the Stooges wreaked havoc on each other. In their own way they were doing their part to help the country forget its mid-Depression blues.

Pop Goes the Easel, *1935*.

Uncivil Warriors, *1935*.

Pardon My Scotch, *1935*.

Three Little Beers, *1935*.

Hoi Polloi, *1935*.

Restless Knights

About the Film

Restless Knights (Prod. No. 160), the Stooges' sixth short, was released on February 20th, 1935. This is one of the few scripts that, for reasons unknown, was not in my father's collection. Luckily, I was able to get special permission from Columbia Pictures to make a photocopy of the script which was on file in the library at the Academy of Motion Picture Arts and Sciences as part of their Jules White Collection.

When you have the opportunity to watch a Stooges film frame by frame as I have, trying to pick the best ones in order to illustrate a book, you find yourself scrutinizing the film and noticing certain things other than the dialogue, gags and crazy action. While sitting back and enjoying this silly comedy, I immediately noticed the high quality of the production—the elaborate sets and expensive costumes. I was perplexed at first as to why Columbia would go to such expense on a low-budget Stooges comedy, and then I recalled an article written by Elwood Ullman on the very subject. I pulled it from my files and found the following quote by this prolific writer of Stooges comedies.

"I'd be at my desk perusing *Variety,*" wrote Elwood, "when the boss, Jules White, might buzz me and say, 'There's an English manor set on Stage Two that's available to us. Take a

Line drawing made from a photograph from Restless Knights *by an unknown artist.*

stroll through there and see if you can come up with a story idea for the Stooges that would fit the set.' "

During my research I learned that the Stooges used many of the elaborate sets from Columbia's major motion pictures. They would take advantage of that interim period after the production was completed but before the sets were torn down to make more stage space available. But the sets for *Restless Knights* puzzled me, as I had no idea what major feature they were originally constructed for.

As my husband constantly told me, research is like detective work, so my next move was to speak to Dennis Doph, the head of Columbia Pictures Non-Theatrical/Classics. Dennis knows everything there is to know about all Columbia's vintage motion pictures and has a

vast library of prints at his fingertips. I called him and asked if he could recall a film produced by Columbia back in 1934 or 1935 that might have sets reminiscent of *Restless Knights*. I didn't have long to wait; that same afternoon Dennis called back with the information I needed. He explained that Columbia made very few period films and the only one that it could possibly be was *The Black Room,* which starred Boris Karloff.

Among the production stills for *Restless Knights* were several 8 × 10's which had nothing whatsoever to do with the story and which contained props that never appeared in the film. For example, the giant toy horse that appeared in one still photo was used strictly for promotional purposes.

In carefully going through the individual frames of *Restless Knights,* I also discovered

Boris Karloff in a scene from The Black Room, *the film from which the sets for* Restless Knights *were taken.*

the use of doubles. In the wrestling sequence, where Curly appears to spin Larry through the air, then tosses him off scene where he lands on the queen's throne with her crown on his head, I came across several frames containing either dummies or doubles. Special effects in Stooges comedies were all done on the set, and in this scene they used a combination of a dummy, a wire gag and a man who acted as a double for Larry. Finally, with some very clever editing, the entire mish-mash was made to work. The frames I chose should give one some idea of how the end result was achieved.

Not having checked the cast sheet before I started my frame selection, it took my husband Norman to recognize the bearded old man in the opening scene as Walter Brennan. When Brennan spoke his first line, there was no doubt that Norman was right.

The film pretty much follows the script's story line up until the ending, which is radically different. In the final scenes of the film, the Stooges free the queen and in a crazy routine in the castle's corridors, trying to wipe out the guards who are chasing them, they wind up smashing the queen over the head. Realizing what they have done, they bop one another over the head as the film FADES OUT. In the script, however, we have a very expensive free-for-all between the Stooges, Count Boris and six of his men. In an attempt to escape, the Stooges shove a wine hose into Boris's mouth and pump him full of wine. They do this to Boris's men also, and the chaos intensifies as the whole group staggers about helplessly. Finally, the Stooges are praised by the queen for a job well done and asked to kiss her hand. The scene ends with Curly's dialogue, "Boo woo woo" instead of "Woo woo woo," and the line, "It's an old Spanish custom." Larry and Moe, who think they are kissing the queen's hand are actually kissing one another's. On this action we FADE OUT:

I can well understand the producer's not wanting to use the script's ending. Although it was an action-packed one, it was also a very costly one to film.

As far as finding reviews on *Restless Knights,* I spent several hours at the Margaret Herrick Library searching through old issues of the *Motion Picture Herald* and *Variety* and came up empty-handed. For this reason, my opinion will have to suffice.

Although not the best of Stooges comedies, this film was chosen for the lavish costumes and sets and because it was one of the three films on Volume IX of the Three Stooges video cassettes, which makes the cassette compati-

ble with this book. After screening the film several times, I found the pacing slow and the story nil. I have always enjoyed a Stooges short better when the comedy evolves from the story points, and this film certainly does not meet that requirement. As my father explained to a multitude of reporters, the Stooges' formula for the two-reelers would always be to ask the question, "Where would we be most out of place?" And on that premise the writers would create a story. *Restless Knights* held to that formula and the Stooges certainly looked out of place as the Three Musketeers performing their kooky swordplay and crazy slapstick action.

In summation, *Restless Knights* as a Stooge Comedy is far from being one of their classic shorts but, because of its action, sets and production values, it lent itself well to being illustrated here.

The Stars

Curly
(Baron of Gray Matter)

Moe
(Count of Fife)

Larry
(Duke of Durham)

The Cast

GENEVA MITCHELL
(Queen)

WALTER BRENNAN
(Father)

GEORGE BAXTER
(Count Boris)

WILLIAM S. BLYSTONE
(Captain of the Guards)

73

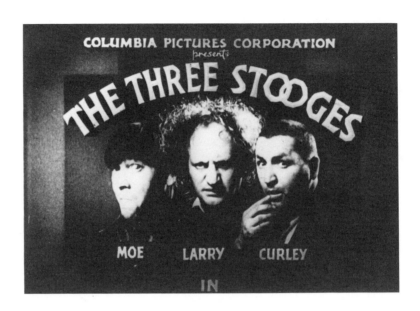

in

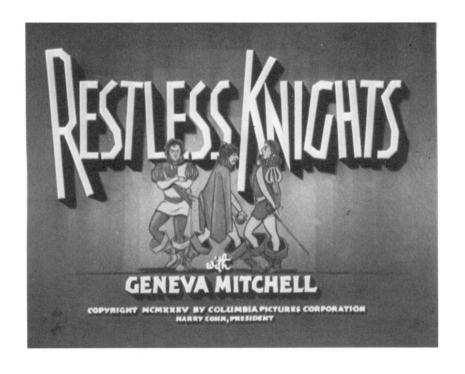

74

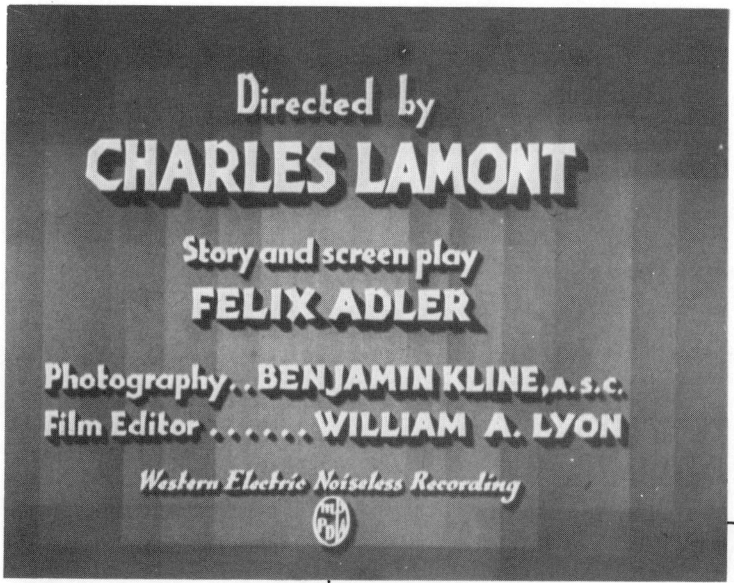
Directed by
CHARLES LAMONT
Story and screen play
FELIX ADLER
Photography . . BENJAMIN KLINE, A.S.C.
Film Editor . . . . . . WILLIAM A. LYON
Western Electric Noiseless Recording

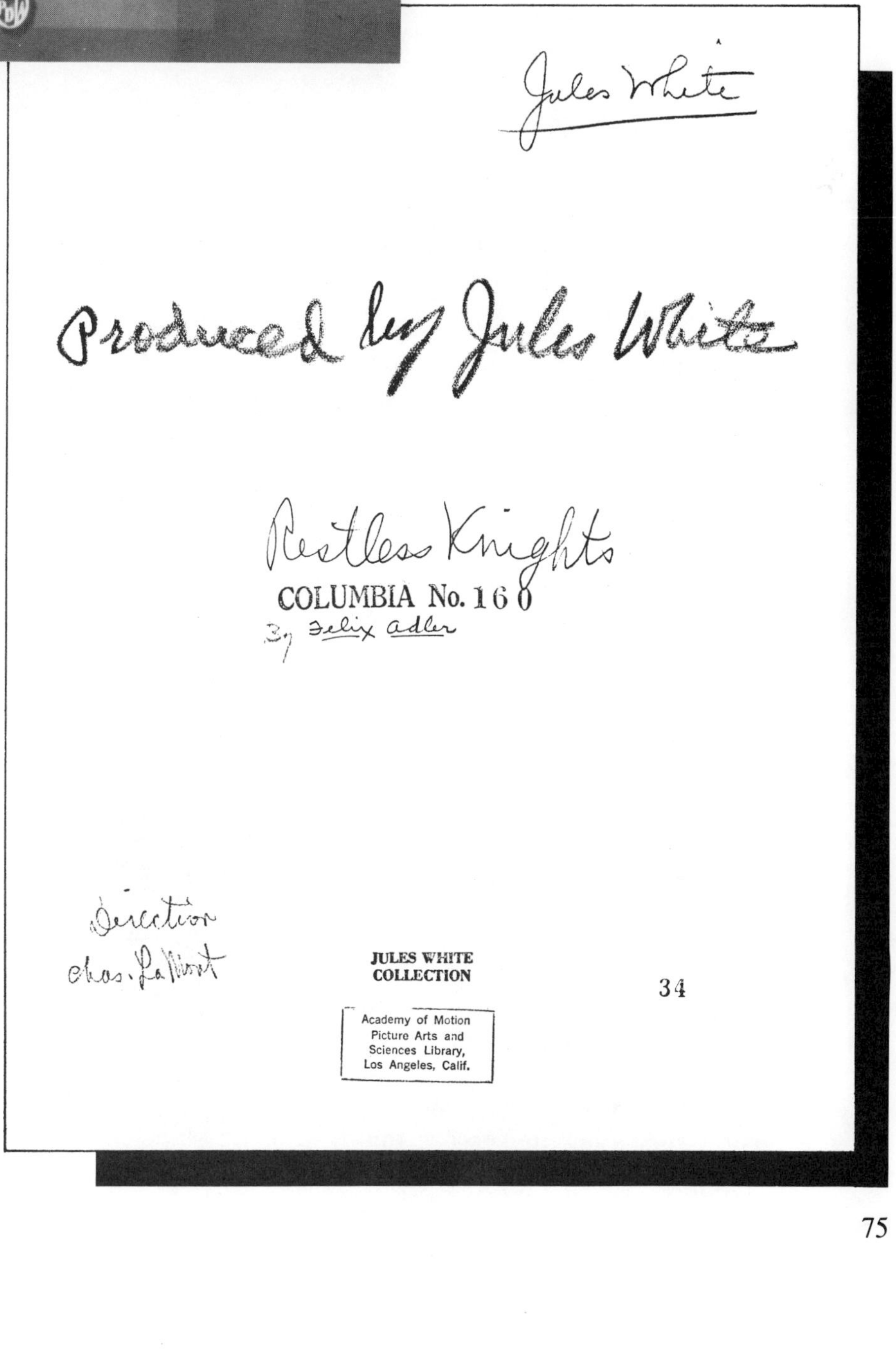

Jules White

Produced by Jules White

Restless Knights
COLUMBIA No. 160
By Felix Adler

Direction
Chas. LaMont

JULES WHITE
COLLECTION

34

FOREWORD
IN THE SIXTEENTH CENTURY INTRIGUE RAN RAMPANT
AND TO THE VICTIM BELONGED THE SPOILED"

1.

1   FADE IN:
     INTERIOR OF BEDROOM (NIGHT) FULL SHOT

     This is the kind of bedroom that was in vogue in the
     Sixteenth Century - not too gaudy. It is dimly lighted by
     a large candle near the bedside. In the bed, an old man
     with a long, flowing white beard is lying while an attendant
     administers aid. Outside the windows a storm is seen raging,
     the rain coming down in torrents with intermittent flashes
     of lightening and peals of thunder.

     DOLLY TO CLOSER SHOT AT BED

     The old man is very weak and in a shaking voice he speaks
     to the attendant.

                         OLD MAN
               Call my sons! ... I would speak with them,
               and this wild, tempest-laden night suits with
               the purpose best.

     The attendant nods and turns away.

2   MEDIUM SHOT

     As the attendant opens the door a gust of air blows in on
     him, causing his clothing to flutter.

3   CLOSE SHOT OLD MAN IN BED

     The air blows the old man's whiskers up around his face.
     He has difficulty in getting them down, then feebly tucks
     them under the covers so they won't blow up again.

4   ANGLE AT DOOR

     Into the room comes the three stooges, in nightgowns. They
     each carry a lighted candle of different sizes, lighting
     the room to a brighter glow.

     PAN WITH THEM

     as they cross to the old man's bedside, bow reverently, and
     say,

                         STOOGES
                       (In unison)
               Hey - nonny, nonny!

The Curly line on script page #1 was
changed from, "Hey, nonny nonny" to
"Hi'ya, pop!" The words "Hey, nonny
nonny and a hot cha-cha," were part of
the lyrics of a very popular song from the
thirties. The writer attempted to use this
line three separate times in the script.

76

The opening location in the script *Restless Knights* is INT. BEDROOM. Since it is difficult to set a scene with an interior shot, "stock film" (existing film from another picture) was added, depicting an old castle over which rain was superimposed. When the sound effect of thunder was added, this was truly, "a wild, tempest-laden night" as described in the script's dialogue.

The Old Man's dialogue on script page #1 was changed in the film as our dialogue balloon indicates. I believe the change was made due to the awkward wording in the script, and the addition of the word "with" in the dialogue makes absolutely no sense.

This scene in the script was changed from the Stooges entering the bedroom with lighted candles to one with Curly popping out from under the covers and Moe and Larry from under the bed. The action must have been ad-libbed on the set during rehearsal and is certainly a much more humorous entrance for the Stooges.

77

5   <u>ANGLE ON OLD MAN & STOOGES</u>

He starts to sit up, to speak to them and as he does his whiskers come from under the covers and blow around his face. The three boys come to the rescue and put the whisker back under the covers again. The old man sighs and speaks i a feeble voice.

                    OLD MAN
          Gather closely, sons, I have a terrible
          confession to make.

6   <u>CLOSE SHOT OF STOOGES</u>

They take this in fear, exchange quick glances then bend over the old man.

7   <u>ANGLE ON OLD MAN & CURLY</u>

As Curly bends over to listen, the hot tallow from his candle drops on the old man's forehead. He lets out a feeble squawk and with a trembling hand pulls the tallow from his forehead and throws it in Curly's face. Curly reacts in his pansy manner.

8   <u>ANGLE ON GROUP</u>

                    MOE
          Go ahead, pop, and spill the porridge.

                    OLD MAN
          Listen, sons --- you must know the truth -
          you ---

                    BOYS
             (In unison - eagerly)
          Yes?

                    OLD MAN
          You --

                    BOYS
             (In unison - eagerly)
          Yes?

                    OLD MAN
          (Dropping his voice to hoarse
           whisper)
          You are of ---
           (voice still lower)
          - - of Royal blood!
              Noble Birth

9   <u>CLOSE SHOT STOOGES</u>

They react in surprise, then Larry says ..

                    LARRY
          Ah, ha! So you've been holding out on us!

10   ANGLE ON GROUP

The old man sits up in bed and the whiskers fly up in his
face again. Moe grabs them and holds them down as the old
man speaks.

                    OLD MAN
        Years ago I was the Royal Chamberlain of the
        Kingdom of Anesthesia.

                    CURLY
        And mama?

                    OLD MAN
        She was the Royal Chambermaid. For marrying
        her I was banished and became an outcast.

                    MOE
        And now we're taking pot luck.

11   ANGLE ON OLD MAN

His eyes grow wide as he says in a frightened voice.

                    OLD MAN
        Our old Kingdom is in danger. The present
        Prime Minister is plotting to either oust or kill
        our young queen!

12   ANGLE ON STOOGES

They look at one another quickly, then Larry asks ..

                    LARRY
        What can we do?

The old man moves restlessly, pulling his whiskers from
Moe's grasp. They fly up around his face again. Moe
sees a bag with a draw string on it and taking it he
tucks the old man's whiskers into the bag.

13   ANGLE ON OLD MAN

Getting the whiskers into the bag, Moe pulls the draw
string tight as the old man says ..

                    OLD MAN
        Offer your swords in the Queen's service.

14   ANGLE ON STOOGES

They laugh at this. The old man points a shaking finger
at Larry.

It is interesting to note that the second "Hey, nonny nonny" was crossed out in the script and the "All for one and one for all" line was inserted in pencil onto the script page. This line is the one that appears in the finished film. Another note was written in the margin on script page #4 regarding the word "huddle" which refers to the football huddle used in the

80

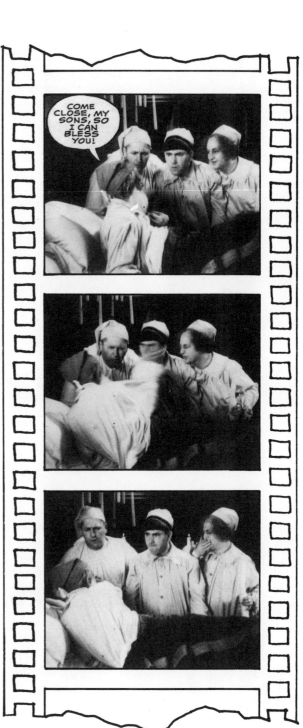

Stooges' vaudeville act. This silly bit of business was also used in the short *Men in Black*, as well as in many other Stooges comedies.

> OLD MAN
> You are rightfully the Duke of Durham!
> (Pointing at Moe)
> You are the Count of Fife!

> CURLY
> (Speaking out of turn)
> And I'm the Count of Ten!

Moe takes it, giving him a slap as the Old Man continues...

> OLD MAN
> No - you are Baron of Gray Matter!

15   <u>CLOSE UP CURLY</u>

looks at him happily flattered - then he realizes the
meaning - reacts.

16   <u>CLOSE UP MOE</u>

> MOE
> Father, we shall do your bidding!

They bow low to the old man. Moe bops Curly on the forehead.

17   <u>CLOSE SHOT ON GROUP</u>

The old man rises to a sitting position.

> OLD MAN
> Come close, that I may bless you.

They come close and lean over. He gives them the tripple
slap.

18   <u>MEDIUM SHOT</u>

The attendant enters the scene with a goblet of steaming
liquid and hands it to the old man who indicates the door
to his sons.

> OLD MAN
> Go, my sons -- and leave me to my fate!

The boys bow out very reverently as the old man raises the
goblet to his lips.

> STOOGES
> (In unison)
> Hey, nonny nonny!

[handwritten: Huddle one for all etc]

[handwritten: one for all — all for one — Every one for himself]

Three time Academy Award winner Walter Brennan gives the *triple* slap to the *Three* Stooges. It goes to show you that everything happens in threes.

18   CONTINUED   5.

      Old Man lowers the goblet and smacks his lips as he
      replies ..

                         OLD MAN
            Hot - cha - cha!

                                             FADE OUT

19   FADE IN
      INT. GORGEOUS THRONE ROOM (DAY) FULL SHOT

      Members of the Court, both male and female, are gathered
      mid pomp and splendor. At one end or side of the room is
      the Royal chair. Heralds standing in the arch to the room
      come to attention and with their trumpets to their lips
      blow a sour fanfare. The Royal Announcer calls out ..

                         ROYAL ANNOUNCER
            His Highness - Prince Boris, Prime Minister
            of Anesthesia!

      Through the arch comes Boris, followed by his bodyguard.

20   ANGLE AT ARCH

      Boris pauses and looks over the room arrogantly, then
      starts toward the Throne chair.

      CAMERA DOLLYS WITH HIM

      and as he passes the guest they bow. He takes his place
      beside the throne chair and faces the arch. As he does,
      another fanfare of trumpets is heard. (Like musical
      auto horn) - toot - to - to - to -

21   FULL SHOT

      As the attendants lower their trumpets the Royal Announcer
      calls out.

                         ROYAL ANNOUNCER
            Her most gracious and regal majesty--
            Our own Queen Ann of Anesthesia!

22   CLOSE SHOT AT ARCH

      The Queen, a very beautiful young girl, makes her entrance,
      accompanied by her ladies in waiting who carry her train.
      She pauses and smiles over the assembly, then starts toward
      her throne.

      CAMERA TRUCKS WITH HER

The opulent sets and the elegant costumes in the photographs on this page go to prove that my research was correct—that many of the elaborate sets found in Stooges comedies were used to improve production values and were borrowed from Columbia's major features. In the throne room scene we see the set and costumes from the Boris Karloff film *The Dark Room*.

22   CONTINUED   6.

       and as she passes the guests they drop to one knee and pay
       her homage. During the procession, the trumpets blast forth
       lusty march. Reaching the throne she turns and faces the
       people.

23   CLOSE SHOT OF QUEEN AT CHAIR

       With a gracious wave of her hand she speaks.

                              QUEEN
                    We bid you rise!

24   FULL SHOT OF THRONE ROOM

       The people rise to their feet. As they do, the Announcer
       enters and hurries toward the queen.

25   ANGLE ON QUEEN ON THRONE

       The announcer enters, drops to one knee and salutes the
       Queen, then says ..

                              ANNCUNCER
                    Three gentlemen of noble birth and mein
                    desire an audience with Your Majesty.

                              QUEEN
                    Who are they?

                              ANNOUNCER
                    From what they say, I gather they are the
                    Duke of Mixturo, the Fife of Drum and
                    Baron of Brains!

                              QUEEN
                    Call the guards!

                              ANNOUNCER
                         (To assembly)
                    Calling all guards!

       Voices pick up off scene --

                              VOICE
                    Calling all guards!

                              ANOTHER VOICE
                    Calling all guards!

       This is carried on so that it sounds like the radio police
       call -- "Calling all cars."

26 <u>FULL SHOT</u>

Through the arch comes a skinny wheezened individual in knickers and armour. He runs to the queen's throne and salutes.

27 <u>CLOSE SHOT OF MAN</u>

As he talks, his adams apple works up and down.

        MAN
    Did you call me, your Majesty?

28 <u>ANGLE ON QUEEN</u>

         QUEEN
    Yes!
      (To the announcer)
    Bid the tree strangers enter!

The announcer runs out.

29 <u>FULL SHOT</u>

Into the throne room comes the tree stoges.* They are at-tired in costumes resembling the Three Musketeers, their swords, without scabbards, shoved through their belts. They start toward the queen.

30 <u>MEDIUM SHOT AT THRONE</u>

There is a large throw rug in front of the throne and as the Stooges hurry up and step on the rug it slides with them, causing them to fall in front of the Queen, the guests gasp.

31 <u>CLOSE SHOT STOGGES</u> *

As they pick themselves up their swords are seen to be bent out of shape like corkscrews. They go into a huddle then drop to one knee before the Queen.

32 <u>ANGLE ON STOOGES</u>

Moe, seeing that Larry and Curly are not resting on the right knee, gives them the slap and working over, saying ..

        MOE
    Varlets! The wrong knee!

The two boys correct their position.

* How does one spell Stooge?

BID THE THREE STRANGERS ENTER!

DID YOU CALL ME, YOUR MAJESTY?

33   <u>MEDIUM SHOT</u>

                         QUEEN
                  Arise!

      The boys get up.

                         QUEEN
                  From whence came you?

34   <u>ANGLE ON STOOGES</u>

                         LARRY
                  Paris!

                         CURLY
                  Show her the postal cards.

                         QUEEN
                  What were you doing in Paris?

                         MOE
                  Looking over the parasites!

                         QUEEN
                  What brings you here?

      The three stooges draw their bent swords and extend them
      toward the queen, saying in unison ..

                         STOOGES
                  To offer our swords in your service!

35   <u>ANGLE ON QUEEN</u>

      She looks at them in surprise.

                         QUEEN
                  Why?

36   <u>ANGLE ON STOOGES</u>

      Moe leans toward the queen confidentially.

                         MOE
                  (Lowering his voice)
                  There are rumors of intrigue against
                  your Majesty.

                         LARRY
                  We will guard you well, Annie.

The film frame with the Stooges holding kooky, twisted swords and which I have used to illustrate script page #9, has them delivering the lines, "All for one, one for all and I'll take care of myself." This was the pay-off for the earlier handwritten line on script page #4.

```
36      CONTINUED                                        9.
                                    MOE
                              (Slapping him)
                        Queenie to you!

37      CLOSE ON QUEEN

        She smiles at them.
                                    QUEEN
                        We accept your offer and appoint you
                        the Queen's Royal  Guards!

38      MEDIUM SHOT

        The boys shove  their swords back into their belts and bow,
        exclaiming ..
                                    STOOGES
                        Hey, nonny nonny!

        Boris steps to the queen, saying ..

                                    BORIS
                        Your Majesty, the royal wrestlers await you!

        He extends his hand to help the queen up.  As he does, the
        Stooges turn away from the Queen.

39      ANGLE ON STOOGES AT THRONE

        As they turn, they see three of the Queen's ladies in
        waiting approaching and with big smiles they bow deeply
        to them.  As they doff their hats, they slap each other in
        the fact with them.

40      ANGLE ON BORIS AND QUEEN

        He is bending over, offering the queen his hand to help her
        from the throne as the Stooges bow and their swords stick
        him in the fanny.  He lets out a yell and jumps, throwing
        his arms around the queen, who gives a startled little
        scream.

41      MEDIUM SHOT

        The Stooges turn quickly at the Queen's scream, see Boris
        with his arms around the queen and grab him from her, throw-
        ing him to the floor, then each placing a foot on him they
        turn to the queen.
```

                    CURLY

        BOO woo woo!
                            LARRY
        Quick work, hey Annie?

                            MOE
        Best running guards in the Kingdom, huh,
        Queenie?
                            QUEEN
        Very good, but come - let us ~~away to~~ _Watch_ the
        Wrestling Match.

                                                WIPE OUT

42   INT. PALACE AMUSEMENT R OM (DAY) FULL SHOT

        In the middle of the room, on a fancy mat, two wrestlers
        are in the midst of combat. One of them is a huge fellow
        with a big bushy beard (a la Dean) while the other is a
        much smaller man. The members of the court are gathered
        around, sitting and standing as they watch the match. At
        one side of the room, in front of a draped window or archway
        the Queen is seated on a throne, the three Stooges beside
        her, Boris nearby.

43   ANGLE ON WRESTLERS

        They grunt and heave at each other as they do a legitimate
        wrestling act.

44   ANGLE ON THREE STOOGES

                        MOE

        I'll bet on the little guy!

                        LARRY
        How much?

                        MOE
        Three thousand guineas, two geese and one
        duck!

                        CURLY
        Throw in a chicken and I'll take half of
        it!

45   ANGLE ON WRESTLERS

The wrestling continues and one of the men with a
series of grips and body slams vanquishes his opponent,
places his foot on the loser's chest awaiting the
plaudits of the Queen.

46   ANGLE ON QUEEN

She smiles approval and tosses a sack of gold to the
victorious wrestler.

47   ANGLE ON QUEEN & STOOGES

Curly scoffs ..

                    CURLY
          Poo poo! That's nothing!

                    LARRY
          It's a frame up!

                    MOE
          Queenie --
              (Points at Curly)
          he's got the strongest feet in the
          Kingdom!

                    QUEEN
              (Indicating mat)

          I would see you perform!

                    MOE
          Keep a stiff upper lip, Queenie. We'll
          be back in a jiffy.

They exit.

                                        WIPE CUT

This 8 × 10 still was used not only for one-sheets and lobby cards but also for newspaper publicity.

48   WIPE IN
      INT. ANOTHER ROOM OF PALACE (DAY) MED. LONG SHOT

      The Stooges enter the room attired in oversized, old
      fashion bathing suits. They approach the mat. Moe and
      Curly are wrestlers while Larry acts as referree. Larry
      calls them to the center of the mat and examines their
      finger nails. He sees a nail on Curly's hand that is too
      long and bites it off, then tells them to get ready.

                            LARRY
                  Get ready!

      As they start to walk away, Moe accidentally bumps Curly
      and Curly falls fl at on his back. They pick him up.

                                            CUT TO

49   MED. CLOSE SHOT QUEEN AND GROUP OF SPECTATORS

      They watch the proceedings.

                                            CUT TO

50   WRESTLING MAT .. MED. SHOT

      Curly and Moe face each other menacingly. As they ap-
      proach each other, each puts his hands on the others
      shoulders. As they maneuver for position they each go
      faster and faster until finally they stop with a grip
      on the back of each other's neck. Quickly they begin
      to massage each other's head.

51   CLOSE SHOT MOE AND CURLY

      As they massage each others heads. Suddenly, Moe slaps
      Curly away from him.

52   MEDIUM LONG SHOT

      Curly and Moe square off toward each other and rush in.
      They grapple in a handshake grip, each trying to move
      the other. Finally, Moe gets Curly's hand up into the air.
      They go into a Minuet. They continue the Minuet to a fin-
      ish then bow to each other. As Curly bows, Moe socks him
      on the head. Curly comes up with his hands on his hips,
      sore as the devil.

53   MEDIUM CLOSE SHOT

      They square off and glare at each other, then start toward
      each other menacingly.

Many areas in the wrestling sequence, although scripted, do not match the film. I imagine director Charles Lamont would not have said, "I made them [the Stooges] follow the script—I was never a great admirer of ad-libs," if he had realized this. If you compare script to film you will see Curly tossing Larry off scene instead of Moe as the script called for.

I got a laugh out of the film frame where Curly and Moe are scratching each others heads and Larry is in the background, seated in a chair fast asleep. He is either a very relaxed actor or bored with Moe's and Curly's shennanigans.

54   MEDIUM LONG SHOT

As they start toward each other menacingly, Curly has his
arms upraised over his head a la Mephisto. He frightens
Moe who sinks to his knees on the mat. As Curly bends
over Moe menacingly, Moe sneezes in Curly's face. Curly
reacts and retreats. Larry comes up to warn Moe. Moe
sneezes in Larry's face. Larry picks up a bathtowel, rubbing himself as though he had just taken a bath -- around
the back, down the arms, around the legs, etc.

(GET CLOSEUPS OF FOREGOING ACTIONS)

                                                    CUT TO

55   MED. C. S. QUEEN AND GROUP

as they watch the wrestling antics.

                                                    CUT TO

56   WRESTLING MAT ... MEDIUM SHOT

Moe and Curly face each other. They go into a routine of
arm movements which end up with them doing wig wag signals
like sailors, then they advance to each other, embrace
and kiss like Frenchmen. Curly again bows, Moe slaps him
on the back of the neck with his gripped hands, flooring
Curly. Curly gets up sore as the devil and starts to walk
away.

                        CURLY
            I quit!

As he approaches Larry, Larry slaps him in the face and
says ..

                        LARRY
            Get back in there and fight, you coward!

57   CLOSEUP OF CURLY

He reacts to this ...

                        CURLY
            Boo woo woo!

rubbing his face, etc., then turns toward Moe with a
murderous expression.

58   CLOSEUP OF MOE

He lowers his head like a goat.

MEDIUM LONG SHOT   14.

Moe squares off as Larry comes in behind him. Moe takes
a run at Curly, butts him in the stomach and bounces back,
bumping into Larry and flooring him. Quick as a flash, Moe
turns, pounces on Larry, gets head locks, toe holds, etc. on
him, almost tearing him to pieces, until finally he has
Larry out cold. Curly approaches Moe, pats him on the back,
Moe gets up and Curly raises Moe's hand.

(GET CLOSEUPS OF FOREGOING ACTION)

60   CLOSEUP OF CURLY AND MOE

Curly has Moe's arm raised. Moe bows a couple of times,
suddenly realizes that Curly is the one he should be
wrestling with as Curly reacts at the same time and they
quickly begin to wrestle.

61   MEDIUM LONG SHOT

Moe has Curly's arm upraised. They recognize each other and
start to wrestle. Moe turns quickly, pulling Curly over his
shoulder in a body slam, throwing him to the mat. Curly
lands on his stomach; Moe pounces on him, lifts Curly's arm
and pulls the hair under his arm, then quick as a flash
begins to massage Curly. Curly lays there and likes it.
He pantomines for Moe to scratch his back up higher. Moe
complies, then realizes what he is doing. Angrily, he turns
Curly over and they wrestle.

                                                   CUT TO

62   MED. SHOT QUEEN AND GROUP

as they watch the wrestling.

                                                   CUT TO

63   CLOSEUP BORIS AND HENCHMEN (yet another)

They are in back of the Queen's throne where they cannot
be overheard.

                         BORIS
               Now is your chance. Seize the queen
               and do away with her and I will take
               charge of the Kingdom.

The men nod and Boris turns away, exiting from the scene.

63 CONTINUED:

PAN WITH THE MEN as they sneak toward the queen, one of
them claps his hands over her mouth and they both pick her
up and drag her behind the drapes in back of the throne.
In tho tussle, the Queen's crown is left behind, stuck on
the arm of the throne.

WRESTLING MAT

64 MED. CLOSE SHOT
Moe has Curly down. He is trying to force one last
shoulder down and Curly resists subbornly. Larry comes in,
gets on his hands and knees, sticks his head right under
the upraised shoulder, trying to see how far Curly is from
being down. Moe, witha lightning like movement, forces
Curly's elbow down, slamming Larry on the side of the
face. Larry goes out like a light. Moe and Curly continue the action of trying to get the shoulder down.
Larry begins to come to. Just then, Moe again forcefully
slams Curly's arm down, the elbow again knocking Larry
cold. Suddenly, Moe whirls and pounces on top of Curly.

65 MEDIUM SHOT - ANOTHER ANGLE
Moe gets Curly's shoulder and forces it down, but the
prostrate Larry, out cold under the shoulder, prevents Moe
from downing Curly. After a couple of attempts Moe
furiously jumps to his feet. He picks Larry up by one
arm and one foot, whirls him a la Adagio and tosses him to
Curly who has gotten to his feet. Curly catches Larry and
continues to whirl him around a la Adagio, then tosses him
back to Moe who catches him, does a couple more spins and
throws Larry out of the set.

EMPTY THRONE

66 MEDIUM SHOT
The people are interested in watching the wrestling match
as Larry (double) flies in and lands in the throne in a
sitting posture.

67 CLOSEUP LARRY IN THRONE
Larry sits up goofily and the crown drops on his head in a
funny position.

68 MED. LONG SHOT
As the assembly turns and sees Larry in the throne they
react in surprise and everyone exclaims.

                    VOICES
        The queen! The queen! Where is the
        queen?

It is interesting to note how special effects were done in the thirties. In this sequence Curly is supposed to toss Larry out of the scene. In order to do this, first he swings a dummy up into the air which is supposed to look like Larry. In the next cut, a man (Larry's double) hurtles through the scene on a wire and lands on the throne. Cut again and we see a close-up of Larry on the throne with a dazed look on his face and the queen's crown on his head. These separate scenes are then edited to-gether and on-screen you'd swear that Curly tossed Larry o.s. and that Larry sailed into the scene, landing on the throne.

In the film frame at the top right-hand side of the page, the Stooges catch three swords that fly into the scene. In this bit of trickery, the swords, which had wires attached to them, were yanked out of the Stooges hands. When the film is reversed, the Stooges appear to catch the swords in mid-air. The photograph also points up the lavish sets and costumes, borrowed from Columbia's big-budget feature film *The Black Room*.

68   CONTINUED:

                              BORIS
                        (feigning excitement)
            The queen has disappeared!
                        (points at stooges)
            Her guards have been lax!

69   MED. CLOSE SHOT MOE AND CURLY

                              MOE
            We have not, we've been wrestling!

70   MED. LONG SHOT
      Boris indicates the three Stooges.

                              BORIS
                  Seize them, men!

      Several men rush the stooges, Larry by now having jumped
      to his feet and joined the other two. In a gag manner,
      either from the scabbards of spectators or from a coat of
      arms on the wall, the Stooges secure swords. They start
      dueling with the men who have drawn swords and are advanc-
      ing on them. A comedy duel ensues in which the Stooges'
      opponents succeed in cutting the shoulder straps of their
      bathing suits, causing the Stooges to grab their bathing
      suits just in time to keep them from falling. (This is
      to be done one by one so as to get the laughs out of each
      individual) They fight valiantly but are finally over-
      powered.

71   CLOSEUP OF BORIS

                              BORIS
                  Take them away and have them executed!

72   FULL SHOT
      The Stooges are marched out by the soldiers. As they are
      marching out, they turn and shake their fists at Boris,
      forgetting their bathing suits. The bathing suits start
      to fall off and they grab them just in time to keep from
      exposing themselves.

                                        WIPE OFF TO:

EXT. PALACE COURTYARD - DAY

73   FULL SHOT   (Location)
      The three Stooges, dressed in costumes again, are lined
      up against the side of a building. Above them, on the
      first floor of the building, several windows are seen with
      light curtains drawn across them. The boys are facing the
      six guards who have bows and arrows ready, a quiver of

73   CONTINUED:

      arrows hanging at each one's side. A Captain is standing
      beside them, sword in hand.

74   CLOSE SHOT OF STOOGES
      They are looking off toward the guards apprehensively.

75   MEDIUM SHOT
      The Captain raises his sword.

                              CAPTAIN
                    Fix arrows!

      The guards fix the arrows to their bows.

76   CLOSE SHOT OF STOOGES
      (Play this real fast) They shiver in fright. Curly pulls
      out an apple from his pocket and places it on his head.
      Moe sees the apple, takes a bite and puts it back on
      Curly's head. Larry sees the apple, takes a big bite;
      Moe takes another bite, putting back just the core on
      Curly's head. Curly takes what is left of the apple and
      eats it.

77   MEDIUM SHOT

                              CAPTAIN
                    Draw!

      The guards pull back on the bow strings.

78   ANGLE ON STOOGES
      They tremble violently!

                              CAPTAIN'S VOICE
                    Aim!

      They take it fearfully.

79   MEDIUM SHOT
      The Captain is just about to drop his sword and say
      "SHOOT" as Moe calls out.

                              MOE
                    One moment, please!

                              CAPTAIN
                         (to men)
                    As you were!

      The men relax and he speaks to Moe.

79 CONTINUED:

                    CAPTAIN
        What now?

                    MOE
        Isn't there any other way that we
        can die?

                    CAPTAIN
        Yes --

                    CURLY
            (shaking finger at Captain)
        Ah ha! Holding out on us!

                    CAPTAIN
        You can either have your head cut
        off or be burned at the stake.

80 ANGLE ON STOOGES

                    LARRY
        Cut my head off.

                    CURLY
        Not me -- I'd rather be burned at
        the stake!

                    MOE
        Why?

                    CURLY
        Because a hot stake is much better
        than a cold chop!

        Moe slaps him.

81 MEDIUM SHOT

                    CAPTAIN
        Enough of this ribaldry! Draw!

        The men pull back their arrows.

82 ANGLE ON STOOGES
        They take it frightened again.

                    CAPTAIN'S VOICE
        AIM!

                    MOE
        Maybe they'll miss us!

                    CURLY
        That'll be an arrow escape!

In the punch line for this gag where Larry says, "Maybe they'll miss us," Curly answers back, "That'll be an *arrow* escape." It wasn't until today that I figured out the joke. It was impossible to hear this line delivered on the screen, even though I screened it over and over again. I even mis-read the words in the script a dozen times. Now I get it, but I wonder how many people seeing the film got the gag. Did you?

82   CONTINUED:

    He gives a silly little laugh and Moe slaps him. The boys
    all cover their eyes, fearing the end.

83   ANGLE ON CAPTAIN AND MEN
    He is just about to say "SHOOT" again when something above
    the stooges attracts his attention.

84   SHOT OF WINDOW FROM CAPTAIN'S ANGLE (SILHOUETTE)
    A girl in a nightgown has apparently just risen and is
    about to start dressing.

85   ANGLE ON CAPTAIN AND MEN
    The Captain continues to gaze toward the window, everything
    else forgotten. The guard next to him glances at him to
    see why he doesn't say "Shoot", sees the Captain looking
    up and follows his gaze. As he sees what it is he also
    becomes rigid with interest. The guard next to him
    notices his attention and follows his gaze - and so on,
    down the row of guards, until the Captain and his men are
    gazing spellbound toward the window.

86   ANGLE ON THREE STOOGES
    They notice the men's gaze and look up, but being too
    close to the building they can't see in the window. They
    step away from the building, looking up.

87   MEDIUM SHOT
    The stooges step away from the building toward the guards,
    looking up toward the window. As they come up to the
    guards, they finally see what the men are looking at and
    take it with interest.

38   ANGLE ON WINDOW FROM GROUP'S VIEW
    The girl is standing before the window, brushing her hair.

89   ANGLE ON STOOGES
    They continue to watch the window, leaning on some of the
    guards' shoulders to rest themselves.

90   FULL SHOT
    Through a gate in a wall at the rear of the building,
    Boris appears. He sees the men looking up and takes it,
    stepping out in front of them and following their gaze.
    He turns his back to the men the better to see the girl.

91   ANGLE ON GIRL IN WINDOW
    As she starts to take off her nightgown she moves away
    from the window, out of sight.

20.

92   ANGLE ON CAPTAIN
      He snaps out of his trance, sees his men looking up and
      barks at them.

                        CAPTAIN
            Shoot!

      The men release their arrows.

93   ANGLE ON BORIS
      The volley of arrows comes in and hits Boris in the rear.
      He lets out a yell.

94   ANGLE ON CAPTAIN AND MEN
      He takes it startled as he sees what has happened, then
      hurries toward Boris, his men with him. Seeing their
      chance, the Stooges hurry away - run like hell from the
      courtyard.

95   CLOSE SHOT AT WINDOW
      The girl appears with a wash basin of water which she
      empties out the window.

EXT. COURTYARD - DAY

96   ANGLE ON BORIS
      The water comes down and drenches him, which he takes with
      another yell as the Captain and men enter the scene.

                                        WIPE OFF TO:

EXT. LOCATION BESIDE WALL OF ANOTHER BLDG. - DAY

97   The three stooges run in and pause, out of breath.

                        MOE
            If we could only find Queenie -- our
            lives would be spared.

EXT. WINDOW IN BUILDING

98   A hand appears, tossing out a bottle.

99   ANGLE ON STOOGES BESIDE BUILDING
      (N ote: The following action should play fast.) The
      bottle clunks Curly on the head, breaking, and staggering
      him. They take it and look down at the broken bottle and
      see a folded piece of paper. Moe quickly picks it up and
      opens it and reads out loud.

                        MOE
                     (reading)
            "Her majesty is hidden in the wine
            cellars." A friend.

99   CONTINUED:

> CURLY
> (excited)
> Let's go!

> LARRY
> (shaking his head)
> Not me!

> CURLY
> Don't be a fool....even if we don't
> find her, we can get a drink.

As they start away,   CUT TO:

INT. UNDERGROUND WINE CELLAR (DIM LIGHTING)

100   Alongside a huge wine vat the Queen is seen, bound and
      gagged and struggling to free herself. Next to the vat,
      with a hose running into it and another hose running from
      the nozzle, is a large, old-fashioned water hand pump,
      presumably used for pumping out wine.

INT. SMALL UNDERGROUND ROOM

101   Three men are seated around a rough wooden table playing
      cards by candlelight. Each has a bottle of wine at his
      elbow. One of the men picks up his wine and holds it up
      as he says sarcastically.

> MAN
> Long live the queen!

He takes a drink as the other two laugh and one says:

> SECOND MAN
> Boris won't let her live long!

They laugh again.

INT. UNDERGROUND CELLAR - DIRT FLOOR

102   ANGLE TOWARD STAIRS
      Down the steps come the Stooges, each bearing a candle.
      They advance to the middle of the room where there is a
      narrow, backless bench.

> LARRY
> Where is Her Majesty?

> CURLY
> Where's the wine?

Moe gives them a crack, then says:

102   CONTINUED:

Put down your candles!

                        MOE
          Sh! -- There's too much light. Blow
          out your candles!

     Curly and Larry blow out their candles and sit down on the
     bench. Moe crosses toward the wall in back of them.

103   MEDIUM SHOT
      Moe feels along the wall, tapping it and listening to see
      if there is a secret passageway any place, Larry and Curly
      ignore him as they remain on the bench. Bending over, Moe
      lets some of the grease from his candle fall onto the floor,
      then sets the candle in it so it won't tip over. Leaving
      the candle he crosses to the bench, steps over it and SITS
      DOWN BESIDE THE OTHER TWO.

104   ANGLE ON STOOGES
      The candle in back of them near wall.

                        MOE
          We'll map out a plan of campaign.

105   CLOSE SHOT OF CANDLE
      It starts to move and we see that it is fastened to the
      back of a turtle which was resting in a depression in the
      ground, so that its back was level with the dirt floor.

106   ANGLE ON STOOGES
      The candle moves slowly toward them from behind. Moe says:

                        MOE
          The wine-cellar is probably to the
          left.

                        LARRY
          Maybe the treasure vaults are to the
          right.

                                          CUT TO:

INT. WINE CELLAR BESIDE VAT

107   The queen is still struggling with her bonds.

INT. UNDERGROUND CELLAR - STOOGES ON BENCH

108   The candle is close to them. Larry speaks:

                        LARRY
          I think we're hot on the trail.

108   CONTINUED:

                              CURLY
                    You must be mistaken.

109   CLOSE SHOT OF TURTLE
       It crawls under Larry's fanny, the candle close to it as
       Larry's voice is heard.

                          LARRY'S VOICE
                    I'm sure I'm hot!

110   ANGLE ON STOOGES
       As Larry speaks he lets out a yell and leaps to his feet,
       grabbing his fanny. Moe looks up at him angrily.

                              MOE
                    Quiet, you fool! Sit down!

       Larry sits down again. Moe shivers and says:

                              MOE
                    'Tis very cold down here. I wish
                    we had a little heat.

111   CLOSE SHOT OF TURTLE
       It crawls under Moe's fanny as Moe says:

                           MOE'S VOICE
                    I'd give sixteen gilders for a
                    bonfire.

112   ANGLE ON STOOGES
       As Moe speaks, he lets out a yell, then not realizing he
       is the one who yelled he says.

                              MOE
                    Quiet, you fools!

                             CURLY
                    What's the use of sitting around
                    here? Let's start something.

                              MOE
                    Take your time. Let me think!

113   CLOSE SHOT OF TURTLE
       It crawls under Curly's fanny.

114   ANGLE ON STOOGES
       Larry sniffs suspiciously.

114 CONTINUED:

                    LARRY
        I smell rubbish burning.

                    MOE
         (sniffing)
        Maybe somebody's smoking a ham.

Curly lets out a yell:

                    CURLY
        Boo woo woo!

He leaps to his feet, knocking the other two off the
bench.

115 ANGLE ON STOOGES
    As they pick themselves up they react in surprise as they
    see the candle scurry across the floor.

                    CURLY
        The place is haunted!

They run out of set.

INT. UNDERGROUND CORRIDOR (DIM LIGHTING)

116 The three stooges come tiptoeing along, each carrying a
    club of some kind he has picked up. As they reach the
    foreground they pause by a curtained alcove or corridor
    leading off of the one they are in, which has curtains
    across it several feet inside the edge, leaving a small
    nook they could hide in outside the curtains. Moe points
    off down the corridor.

                    MOE
        Look!

117 REVERSE ANGLE DOWN CORRIDOR
    Stooges with backs to camera in f.g. The three men are
    soon playing cards in the small room.

118 ANGLE ON STOOGES

                    MOE
        (to Curly)
        You get their attention, one at a
        time, and let them chase you by here!
         (he indicates the curtained
         cubbyhole)
        We'll do the rest.

118   CONTINUED:

                          CURLY
                     (shaking his head)
               Go chase yourself! I won't go!

Moe slaps Curly - Larry tweeks his nose. Moe gives Curly
the works.

                          MOE
               Now will you go?

                          CURLY
               No, I won't.

They give him more hell.

                          MOE
               Now, will you go?

                          CURLY
               Well, now I'll go.

He exits.

INT. UNDERGROUND ROOM- MEN IN F.G. - DOOR TO CORRIDOR B.G.

119   Curly appears in the door. The fellow who is facing the
       door looks up and sees him. Curly makes a face at him
       and the fellow rises and starts for the door.

INT. CORRIDOR OUTSIDE ROOM

120   Curly retreats down the corridor a few paces and   the
       fellow, drawing his sword, starts after Curly. Curly runs
       down the corridor past the alcove, looking back over his
       shoulder at the fellow who is in hot pursuit. As the
       fellow reaches the alcove the clubs descend on his head
       and he goes limp. Curly pauses and starts back.

INTERIOR CORRIDOR

121   ANGLE AT ALCOVE
       Larry and Moe drag the fellow into the alcove out of
       sight as Curly comes up.

                          CURLY
               How twas? How twas?

                          LARRY
               Fine!

                          MOE
               Fetch the next victim.

Curly starts toward the room.

Script page 26 is radically different from the film. The script must have been running long and it was time to cut, cut, cut. And while they were cutting, another "Hey, nonny nonny" bit the dust.

INT. UNDERGROUND ROOM

122   The two men seated at the table as the sound of a cat
      meowing is heard. (Curly's voice)

                        FELLOW
            Drat that cat!

The meow continues.

                        SECOND FELLOW
            It wants its milk.

The first man gets up and starts for the corridor.

INT. CORRIDOR OUTSIDE UNDERGROUND ROOM

123   The man comes from the room and pauses in surprise as he
      sees Curly meowing. As Curly sees him he makes a face at
      him. The fellow draws his sword and starts after him.

124   ANGLE DOWN CORRIDOR
      Curly repeats the business he did with the first man and
      as he sees him fall he stops and comes back to Larry and
      Moe.

125   ANGLE ON STOOGES AT ALCOVE
      As Larry and Moe drag their second victim out of the way,
      Curly says:

                        CURLY
            Pretty nifty, thinketh not?

                        MOE
            Get the last one!

Curly nods and starts out.

126   ANGLE ON LARRY AND MOE IN ALCOVE
      The curtains part and two sinister figures loom up behind
      the two boys and two clubs descend on their heads and they
      are dragged out of sight.

INT. UNDERGROUND ROOM   *Change to double.*
                                         Sock.
127   Curly appears in the doorway.

                        CURLY
            ~~Hey, nonny nonny!~~

The fellow looks up startled, Curly makes a face at him.
The man scrambles to his feet, overturning the card table,
and drawing his sword starts for Curly.

INTERIOR CORRIDOR

128 Curly repeats his business, looking back over his shoulder
     as the fellow chases after him. As the fellow reaches the
     alcove, Curly slows down, excpecting him to be knocked
     cold. Instead the fellow keeps on coming and taking it in
     alarm Curly puts on a burst of speed and tears around a
     corner of the corridor, the man in hot pursuit.

129 REVERSE ANGLE DOWN CORRIDOR
     Around a corner and down the corridor comes Curly, now
     some distance ahead of his pursuer. He tears around the
     corner out of sight, the man following. HOLD CAMERA IN
     SAME POSITION.

     Curly comes around the corner again and this time he has
     gained so much on the man that he has turned the other
     corner out of sight before the fellow appears. As he
     comes around the corner and down the corridor, Curly
     appears behind him and as the fellow reaches the alcove
     Curly tears up behind him and brings his club down on the
     fellow's head. The fellow stiffens. Curly bats the man
     on the chest. The man goes out of scene backward.

130 MED. CLOSE SHOT - REVERSE ACTION
     The man lands in a corner, standing on his head, his
     feet in the air. Curly puts a vase of flowers on the
     man's upturned feet.

131 CLOSE SHOT CURLY AT ALCOVE
     Tucking his club under his arm, Curly mops his perspiring
     face. As he does, the curtains part and two clubs come
     out and descend on his head, Curly falling to the floor.
     Moe and Larry come out and Moe says to Larry.

                         MOE
              Better late than never.

     They look down and take it in surprise when they see it is
     Curly. Moe quickly gives him a working over on the face
     and he comes to.

INTERIOR WINE CELLAR

132 The queen is just working the gag from her face. She
     screams:

                         QUEEN
              Help! Help!

INT. CORRIDOR AT ALCOVE

133 The stooges react startled as the Queen's voice comes in.

133 CONTINUED:

> QUEEN'S VOICE
> Help! Tis your Majesty needs help!

> BOYS
> 'Tiss off that way. Come!

> QUEEN'S VOICE
> I'm in the wine cellar bound tight!

> MOE
> 'Tis a good place to get tight!

They rush out.

INT. WINE CELLAR

134 MEDIUM SHOT
The Queen still struggling with her bonds as the boys run
in. They quickly free her and she stands up.

135 CLOSE GROUP SHOT

> QUEEN
> You have earned the everlasting
> gratitude of your Queen.

> BORIS' VOICE
> What a pretty sight!

They take it startled and look off.

136 ANGLE AT SIDE OF ROOM
Boris is seen with six of his men. He starts toward them,
drawing his sword. As he does, the Stooges give him a
shove backward into his men, knocking them back. Grabbing
the wine hose, Curly points it at the men as Larry and Moe
man the pump. A stream like a fire hose comes from the
nozzle, knocking the men down and sending them skidding.

137 SHOTS OF MEN
as they slide along floor and bump into wall from force of
wine stream -- the wine staining their clothes and filling
their mouths.

138 ANGLE ON BORIS AND GROUP
Getting up from the floor, Boris makes a rush for the Queen
his sword drawn. Letting go of the pump, Moe grabs a huge
bung starter and smacks him on the head just in time, the
blow sounding loud and hollow. Grabbing a funnel, Larry
shoves it into Boris' mouth and Curly shoves the hose into
the funnel - the force of the wine lessened to a small
stream when they quit pumping.

```
                                                  29.
139   FULL SHOT
      The henchmen, in a drunken condition from the wine, stagger
      to their feet.  The Queen indicates Boris.

                         QUEEN
               Men!

                          MEN
               Yes - hic - your Majesty!

                         QUEEN
               Take him out and behead him immediately!

                          MEN
               Yes - hic - your Majesty!

      They pick Boris up and start out with him as one of them
      says.

                          MAN
               Long live the -- Hic!

140   CLOSE SHOT QUEEN AND STOOGES

                              QUEEN
                 My good men -- I know not how to
                 thank you! -- you may kiss my hand!

      The boys take it, Curly exclaiming:

                          CURLY
               Boo, woo, woo!

      He gives the hose a  flip from him, throwing wine into
      Larry's and Moe's faces, blinding them.

141   TWO SHOT LARRY AND MOE
      They try to wipe the wine from their eyes as they drop to
      their knees and grope for the queen's hand.  A hand comes
      into the scene and they start to kiss it.

142   CLOSE GROUP SHOT
      Curly is standing with one arm around the queen, his other
      hand extended and Larry and Moe are kissing it.  The Queen
      looks at him in surprise and Curly smiles and indicates the
      two boys.

                          CURLY
                 It's an old Spanish custom!

      He leans over as though to kiss the Queen, as we
```

```
                                              FADE OUT

          Tho End
```

In this, the final scene, we find the script very different from the film. While I was looking for more disparities, I came across a line of Curly's dialogue where he is saying, "Boo woo woo" instead of "Woo woo woo." Someone in the stenographic department was certainly not a Stooges fan if they didn't know their woo woos from their boo woos. I found several of these throughout the script.

1939

The Year of
WE WANT OUR MUMMY
and
YES, WE HAVE NO BONANZA

The year 1939 probably produced more great entertainment classics than any other period of movie making. The films ranged from far-out fantasy, *The Wizard of Oz*, to the ultimate in blockbuster period pictures, *Gone With the Wind*, which set an Oscar record in 1939 with eight awards. It was the most expensive, most successful and most discussed movie of the 1930's.

Hollywood reveled in its successful films and elaborate awards festivities while the real world was going through some grave decision-making—the choice between peace or war.

To the surprise and consternation of the world, the Soviet government concluded a non-aggression pact with Germany in which both parties agreed to remain neutral should either one become involved in war. This was interpreted as giving Hitler a free hand in Europe by removing his fear that a European war would have to be fought on two fronts. Hitler ignored England and France's ultimatums to withdraw his armed forces from Poland and on September 3, 1939, England and France declared war on Germany.

With Hitler in the starring role, the world of politics took a turn for the worse while the writers of Stooges comedies took advantage of

The Stooges making like Stooges in a Brooklyn restaurant.

this and started out 1939 with *Three Little Sew and Sews*—a comedy which had the Stooges playing sailors amidst slapstick fun and games with German spies. The remainder of the Stooges comedies in 1939 refrained from playing politics. The writers instead stuck to lighter fare and came up with the fun classics *We Want Our Mummy*, *A Ducking They Did Go*, *Yes, We Have No Bonanza*, *Saved by the Belle*, *Calling All Curs*, *Oily to Bed and Oily to Rise* and *Three Sappy People*.

Although these eight shorts were released throughout 1939, they were all shot before the Stooges left for a personal appearance tour of England and its provinces sometime in late May. The Stooges' tour of England, Scotland and Ireland was a smash hit, but as much as they enjoyed world travel, they were glad to steam out of England on the *Queen Mary* for the return crossing to the States. It was an uneventful trip and was the *Queen Mary's* last voyage before she was converted to a troop ship.

Upon their safe arrival in New York, the Stooges breathed a sigh of relief, having realized as they plowed through the Atlantic's waters that World War II could break out at any moment.

Larry, Moe and Curly went their separate

Moe's residence on Highland Avenue in 1939.

The Stooges during a vaudeville stint with straight man Eddie Laughton.

A telegram to Moe aboard the Queen Mary *from Helen and the children.*

```
□ SA778 B514CC 8B 17 SC
                    LOSANGELES CALIF
    MOE HOWARD
        SS QUEEN MARYPR 90 NR NYK
    GOD BLESS YOU WONDERFUL DADDY ON THIS JOURNEY AND EVER MORE BON
    VOYAGE LOVE FROM YOUR DARLINGS
                            MOTHER JOAN AND PAUL
```

The fourth Stooge in this still is cartoonist George McManus of the world-famous comic strip "Maggie and Jiggs."

THE STOOGES ARE HERE

TOE-STAMPING, brow - slapping comedians of many films, Hollywood's Three Stooges came to Glasgow Empire last night.

They faced an unusually critical audience: screen fans who wondered if these rough-house picture stealers were as funny on the stage as they are before the cameras. I was one of the audience, sharing its doubts.

Thirty seconds after the Stooges came out I was convinced that Hollywood is even crazier than I think in allowing these rough-house boys to leave, even temporarily.

Here is crazy comedy at its best. The familiar brow-slapping, toe-tramping, eye-gouging tricks are all there.

YOU'LL HEAR THEM QUOTE SHAKESPEARE

But the Stooges on the stage add a little choral piece (more of this, please), even a line or two of Shakespeare, and their wisecracks are all exquisitely "insulting."

Before the Stooges we had dusky swingster Ada Brown, billed as "Harlem's Queen of Rhythm." I agree with the billing. I thought Ada wouldn't get off after singing "Some Of These Days," so much did the audience clamour for encores.

More applause for schoolgirl ventriloquist Jennie McAndrew; for jaunty, white-hatted personality singer Jack Daly; for impersonator Billy Nelson and his partner Irene Knight; and for Eddie Laughton (no relation of Charles) for a sophisticated American joke or two.

Full marks, too, for Wee Georgie Wood, short-trousered, plaintively amusing as the little boy wheedling a present for his new girl friend out of his indulgent "mother."

KENNEDY CORCORAN.

Clipping from the Scottish Daily Express *expresses its views on Stooges.*

A program from the Theatre Royal in Dublin, Ireland.

EVENING HERALD

DUBLIN, THURSDAY, JUNE 29, 1939.

PICTURE STORIES OF THE DAY

THE THREE STOOGES and the Zoo elephant provide a humorous picture,

116

Clipping from the Dublin Evening Herald *showing the Stooges during a day at the Dublin Zoo.*

A telegram from comedians Olsen and Johnson during the Stooges' run in George White's Scandals.

Larry and son Johnny vacationing in Florida (1940).

Moe and son Paul, who finally smiles for the camera as he helps his father shave.

ways and my father, together with my mother, my brother and I, got a chance to enjoy the family life we had missed throughout most of the year. This rare time together included several fascinating days at the New York World's Fair, but they were interrupted when the call went out for Moe to join the other two Stooges in Atlantic City to begin rehearsals for *George White's Scandals.* After a hectic tryout, the show opened in New York at the Alvin Theatre on August 28, 1939, lasting for 120 performances and enjoying warm reviews from the press.

One of the Stooges' outstanding comedy routines in the *Scandals* took place on a stage designed to look like a Hollywood movie set, and illustrated how a stand-in does all the dirty work while the film's star takes all the credit. Curly played the stand-in, Larry the star and Moe the irascible director. There were pies by the ton and Curly was at his woo-wooing, whining best.

It was during the *Scandals* run that my father breathed in deeply the sweet smell of success. In order to publicize the Stooges and their Broadway show, a tremendous electronic sign had been built atop a building on Times Square. It consisted of thousands of flashing light bulbs which at night were animated to form a moving silhouette of the Stooges in

action. Thousands of people watched this electrified mayhem as they strolled along Broadway, and years later my father told me that he and my mother stood there one night, admiring

NEW YORK
Herald ✦ Tribune

MUSIC—DANCE
RADIO PROGRAMS

Section
VI

SUNDAY, AUGUST 27, 1939

EIGHT PAGES

...n on Broadway Has Its Overture in Music

George White's Scandals in New Edition

Eugene and Willie Howard, Ann Miller, Ella Logan, Ben Blue and the Three Stooges

As they will appear this week at the Alvin in the first musical of a new season

New Plays of the Week

Tomorrow Night

"SCANDALS," George White's first revue in four years, opens at the Alvin Theater. The cast includes Willie and Eugene Howard, the Three Stooges, Ben Blue, Ella Logan, Ann Miller, Raymond Middleton, Ross Wyse jr., June Mann, Betty Allen and Craig Mathues. Sketches by Matt Brooks, Eddie Davis and George White. Songs by Jack Yellen and Sammy Fain. Scenery by Albert Johnson; Costumes, Charles Le Maire. Mr. White promises a new dance creation, "The Mexiconga."

Hirschfeld cartoon of the stars of George White's Scandals.

A postcard of the Queen Mary—from Moe to Helen.

that brilliant display as Moe, Curly and Larry reenacted their famous eye-poking routine. Lost among the laughing crowd—most of them fans—Moe listened to the remarks of approbation. This is what he had worked so hard for. Then, he told me, he went into the theatre with his heart as light as a feather. The Stooges had become a part of the fabled lights of Times Square and this, according to my father, was the ultimate feeling of success.

In 1939, columnist Kaspar Monahan went to the Stanley Theatre in Pittsburgh to interview the Three Stooges during their vaudeville tour and caught Curly and Larry playing gin rummy in their dressing room. My father was not there when Monahan arrived, so Larry and Curly joked about the rough treatment that Moe gave them. Kiddingly, Curly pointed to a deep scar on one cheek, leading Mr. Monahan to believe that Moe had done it. In reality the scar was the result of an auto accident he was involved in when he was in his twenties and had plowed his parents' Hupmobile into a trolley car, almost snuffing out his life.

Continuing their game during the interview, Larry pointed to a growing bald spot on his head, explaining that for years Moe had pulled out fistfuls of his hair. "But we're not worried," quipped Curly. "When all of Larry's

On the Columbia back lot, Moe, the author and chauffeur Oren Heilman watch Paul drive his custom-built car.

hair is gone—I'll let mine grow back in and he can take over my role and I'll take over his." With Larry and Curly finally cracking up over their little in-jokes, the interview ended. To this day, I wonder whether Monahan actually believed their yarn.

The year 1939 was a big one for Moe. There were not only the continuing Columbia contract, the European tour and the *Scandals*, but the most exciting event of all was in the working stages; an architect was drawing up plans

Mrs. P. Mockler sent this wonderful candid to Joe DeRita who in turn sent it on to me.

While waiting to go on stage, the Stooges sign autographs for one of their fans.

for Moe and Helen's home in the Toluca Lake area of the San Fernando Valley.

Before the completion of our valley home we were living on Highland Avenue in Hollywood during those long-forgotten days when the skies were smogless and the houses were free of iron bars and sophisticated alarm systems.

I recall a very interesting event that happened in the Highland House which always made my father chuckle. It was one that touched on my mother's cousin Harry Houdini. I remember waking up one morning to the sound of raised voices as the maid's excited words rang out, "Mr. Howard, come outside quick—and see what's in the banana tree." When I finally went outside, Mother, Dad and the maid were looking skyward. Silhouetted against a banana leaf was a beautiful green parrot—a full-sized "Polly-wanna-cracker" variety. I arrived just in time to hear the flapping of wings and see the bird take off into the sky.

Everything simmered down after the bird flew away and we all went in for breakfast. This particular morning, my mother had her nose buried in the newspaper. Calm prevailed, until my mother let out a scream and Dad spilled his coffee all over his breakfast. When asked what was the matter, she proceeded to read from the newspaper:

"Betty Houdini, wife of the late Harry Houdini, is staying at the Hollywood Roosevelt Hotel. She is in town for a seance where she hopes to contact her husband, the world-famous escape artist who died in 1927." Mother breathlessly read on: "Mrs. Houdini has been trying to communicate with her dead husband for the past ten years. Always meeting for her seances on Halloween, which is the anniversary of Houdini's death. So far, her efforts have been futile."

The news story hardly raised Dad's eyebrow, but the mess in his plate certainly did— and I couldn't help thinking, "So what?" Not until my mother read the final paragraph of the article did the full extent of her excitement dawn on me. She continued, "Betty Houdini was staying at her hotel in Hollywood and had boarded her pet parrot in a local pet shop. She was heartbroken upon hearing it had escaped."

During a vaudeville stint at the Steel Pier in Atlantic City, we find a seal taking the part of the fourth Stooge.

An interesting still taken during the run of George White's Scandals; *the Stooges are performing their famous "Stand-in" routine.*

121

A bit of trick photography and we have the "Six Stooges."

That pet shop was only three miles from our house and to this day we've always had the eerie feeling that the parrot selected our yard for a perch because it had some connection with Harry's spirit. Many years later, in 1975, that feeling came over me again when my mother passed away—on the anniversary of Harry's death, Halloween.

Early in 1939, while Moe was wrapped up with his family in California, Larry was being dispossessed from his favorite Atlantic City watering hole, the President Hotel, which had been taken over by the United States Army. He was readying himself for the Stooges' European tour and his wife Mabel was upset because she couldn't join him. The thought of traveling by ship, especially with the threat of war, was too much for nervous Mabel, who

had visions of the ship being blown up by a German submarine.

Before Larry left for the tour, an incident occurred which could only have happened in show business. The Stooges, although they weren't the types you could call leading men, had many adoring fans who wrote to them, and one such incident of fan adoration gave Larry a great deal of trouble.

It seems that one day Larry's wife Mabel found a note in his pants pocket from a female fan which read, "Dear Larry: You are a very nice guy and humorous, too. Now, every time I hear the song, 'Thanks for the Memory,' I'll think of you."

Furious with Larry, and certain that there was another woman in his life, Mabel hit him on the head with her shoe. "Thanks for the

What better way to win a war than have the Stooges entertain the troops.

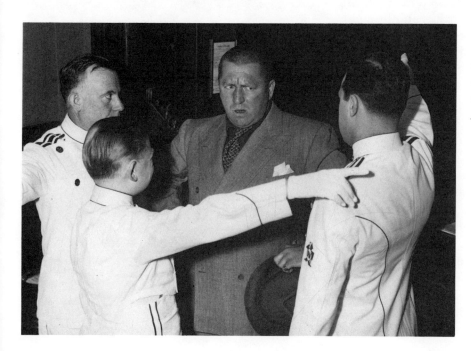

Curly asks directions in London and gets a very confusing answer to "Which way is Trafalgar Square?"

123

Fans Mike and Tom dug up this old candid of Larry—taken on the boardwalk in Atlantic City, 1941.

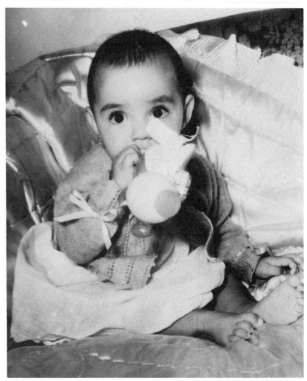

Those teacup-sized eyes staring out at us are Curly's daughter Marilyn's.

Curly and his second wife, Elaine Ackerman, pose for photographs during the announcement of their engagement.

memory!'' she shouted as she threw the note at him. It took quite some time for Mabel to get over this, but after Larry showered her with gifts, which included a goose-egg-sized marquis diamond, the episode was forgotten.

Then, several years later during a tour with the Stooges, Mabel was at ringside watching them perform at a night club when the band started to play "Thanks for the Memory." It was too much for her. She took off her shoe (thank goodness she had dainty little size-3 feet) and threw it at Larry again and ran from the club. My mother ran after her and brought her back. Although the event was once again forgotten, it cost Larry another diamond ring.

While 1938 was one of the high points of Curly's life—the year of a happy marriage and the birth of his daughter Marilyn—the following year, 1939, ended sadly for all the Howard brothers and especially Curly. On September 6, 1939, Moe and Curly's mother, Jennie Horwitz, died. This hit Curly especially hard because he had been around the house the longest and was the closest to her at the time. The fact that his eldest brother Irving had died from appendicitis this same year did not help Curly's mood. Although his career in show business was going well, life in general was a series of trials for my uncle and his mood was pinpointed during a press interview when he made the statement, "Who wants to live long

124

anyway?" Whether said in jest or not, my uncle's words must have reflected some of his innermost thoughts.

Because of this evidence of Curly's sadness, I couldn't help thinking about the relationship between him and other famous comedians of his day who, it was said, lived tragic lives. Maybe it had to do with the fact that comedy is so close to tragedy. The thought fascinated me and, finally, while researching for my book *Curly*, I went to the Margaret Herrick Library at the Academy of Motion Picture Arts and

The author during the summer of 1939, learning to ride.

Sciences and pulled out several biographies on Roscoe "Fatty" Arbuckle, a comedian of the 1920's who became a tragic figure. I put down a lot of basic data and then went home to compare Arbuckle to Curly. I'm sure that this experiment of mine, with only one comparison, does not a theory prove, but the similarites between the two were incredible.

Both Fatty and Curly's lives were brief and sad. Fatty had his notorious trial with accusations of murder, and Curly's life, although nowhere near so sensational, had its moments of bad press and courtroom battles related to his wives. But the similarities do not stop there.

Neither Fatty nor Curly were college graduates. Both their educations were minimal. Curly's took him through grammar school but he did not graduate from high school. Fatty went to Santa Clara High where he is said to have graduated in "football and baseball." Like Fatty, Curly also had a love for sports and both of them were excellent swimmers.

Fatty was the youngest of four children, Curly the youngest of five. The two men watched stage performers when they were young, longing to go into the theatre, and both had beautiful voices. In school their mothers were harassed by teachers about their sons' absence from school. Fatty cut classes to sing ballads in the nickelodeon while Curly played hookey to do a bit of song plugging.

In 1907 Fatty went into vaudeville and made two-reelers. The years were different but Curly did his stint in vaudeville and also made two-reelers. Fatty had three marriages, Curly had four. Fatty was a drinker and giver of wild parties and Curly certainly did his share of both.

As to their physical makeup, both Curly and Fatty had huge, agile bodies and charming cherubic faces. I was very surprised to read that Fatty during his career weighed in at 215. While going through reviews for data on 1939, I came across a clipping in which Curly says, "I'm taking vitamin pills too—to build me up— I only weigh 215."

Fatty had wonderful acrobatic skills and Curly was a fabulous dancer whose graceful flipping around on screen certainly appeared to be an acrobatic skill.

The Stooges during another sketch from George White's Scandals. *Moe would have made a pretty good "Tootsie"?*

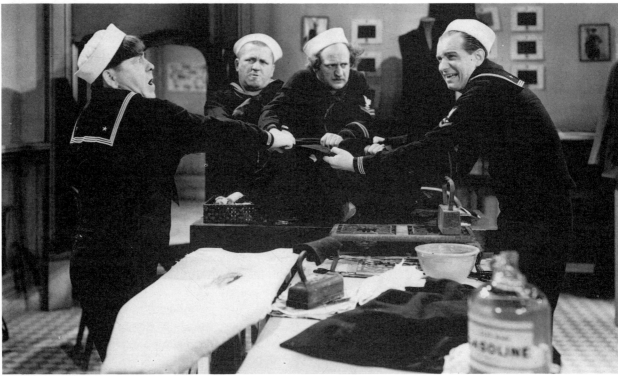

Three Little Sew and Sews, *1939*.

A Ducking They Did Go, *1939*.

Saved by the Belle, *1939*.

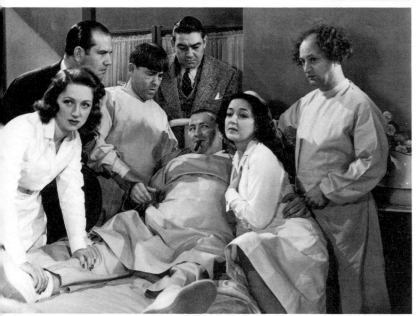

Calling All Curs, *1939*.

And finally, Fatty Arbuckle died of a heart attack at age 46. Curly Howard had a fatal stroke at age 48.

So much for 1939. As Charles Dickens said of another year, "It was the best of times and the worst of times." Certainly that summed up the year for the Three Stooges. They had reached the pinnacle of success and had it tempered with tragedy—both for them personally and for the world around them, a world which had plunged headlong into the cruelest war in the history of mankind.

But the show must go on and, although the Stooges didn't know it then, they would make another 147 slapstick comedies for a world that could use all the cheering up it could possibly get.

Oily to Bed and Oily to Rise, *1939*.

Three Sappy People, *1939*.

WE WANT OUR MUMMY

About the film

On February 24, 1939, Production #443, *We Want Our Mummy,* was released. Again, my choice of this film for the book has to do with the colorful sets, the costumes and the action.

Although *Mummy* was just a romp with no political overtones and very little story, the fact that I visited the set during its production has left me with a special feeling for this film.

I remember that I was twelve and my brother Paul was four. At this point, my film career had ended and it was fun to go back to see what was going on with the Stooges and watch the making of one of their crazy epics.

One particular scene that I recall being shot was the Stooges' arrival by a dusty New York taxi cab at the desert oasis in Egypt. During my stint in Columbia's editing room selecting frames for this book, I came across Curly's line in the film, "Well, being as there is no other place around the place, I reckon this must be the place, I reckon." I realized instantly that I knew that line of dialogue by heart. Curly always had trouble with large blocks of dialogue and I recall him having to repeat this tongue-twister a number of times before he got it right. As always, I became nervous for an actor when he had trouble with his lines and I must have been up-tight myself during the filming of this scene for it to have stuck so indelibly in my memory.

The scene with Curly trying to swim in an imaginary ocean or mirage was my favorite. His facial expressions and body movements were incredible and the grace with which he tossed around his two-hundred-plus pounds was something to see and admire.

Actually, *We Want Our Mummy* had three separate endings which were all somewhat similar. In each one the Stooges ran off in a panic. The first ending with the Stooges running toward their taxi which is mounted on an elephant was apparently much too costly and was discarded. The switch to an alligator enter-

Clipping from a Chicago newspaper dated February 25, 1939, depicting a scene from We Want Our Mummy.

ing the scene and the Stooges taking off in fear, in both the revised script and actual filmed ending, was obviously a prudent move from the standpoint of keeping this Stooges comedy within its skimpy budget.

Although not one of the Stooges' classic comedies, *We Want Our Mummy* had a certain light-hearted charm and was a welcome change of pace from the political satire of *Three Little Sew and Sews,* which preceded it.

The author, Moe and Paul on the set of We Want Our Mummy *(1939) at the Columbia Ranch in Burbank, California.*

The Stars

Curly
(Philo Pants)

Larry
(Sherlock Bones)

Moe
(Charlie Chin)

134

The Cast

BUD JAMISON
(Professor Wilson)

JAMES C. MORTON
(Dr. Crowl)

EDDIE LAUGHTON
(Taxi-Driver)

MUMMY
(Mummy)

DICK CURTIS
(Jackson)

ROBERT WILLIAMS
(Professor Tuttle)

COLUMBIA PICTURES CORPORATION

PRESENTS

THE THREE STOOGES

CURLY   LARRY   MOE

IN

WE WANT OUR MUMMY

Associate Producer
JULES WHITE
Director
DEL LORD

Original Screen Play by
ELWOOD ULLMAN · SEARLE KRAMER

Photography by **ALLEN G. SIEGLER**, A.S.C.
Film Editor **CHARLES NELSON**

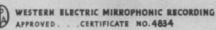

WESTERN ELECTRIC MIRROPHONIC RECORDING
APPROVED . . .CERTIFICATE NO. 4834

STOOGE COMEDY

PRODUCTION #443

By

Searle Kramer
Elwood Ullman

_____

FINAL DRAFT CONTINUITY
OCTOBER 20, 1938

Director
    Del Lord
Producer
    Jules White

STOOGE - PRODUCTION #443

FADE IN: (DAY)

1   CLOSE SHOT - PLAQUE,

      reading: "MUSEUM OF ANCIENT HISTORY
                              Hours 10 to 5"

                                      LAP DISSOLVE TO:

2   CLOSE SHOT - DOOR,

      reading: "EGYPTIAN ROOM." Professor Wilson, an academic
      type, rushes into scene, opens door and enters, CAMERA
      TRUCKING THRU DOOR, following him to:

3   INT. EGYPTIAN ROOM - MED. SHOT

      A dignified looking curator is pacing up and down in front
      of a showcase containing archeological objects; other
      Egyptian trophies in the b.g., getting over the atmosphere
      of the room. Professor Wilson hurries up to the man.

                        PROF. WILSON
          Dr. Crowl - bad news. The police have
          been unable to find even a trace of
          Professor Tuttle! His disappearance
          has them completely baffled.

                        DR. CROWL
          That ruins our hopes of finding the
          Tomb of King Rutentuten. Professor
          Tuttle is the only man alive who knows
          its exact location.

                      PROFESSOR WILSON
           (agitated)
          First Professor Dalton dies mysteriously,
          now Tuttle disappears. Something terrible
          happens to everyone who tries to explore
          that tomb. I tell you it's the curse of
          Rutentuten!

                      DR. CROWL (Pleadingly)
          But unless we secure the mummy of King
          Rutentuten our entire collection is
          worthless. We <u>must</u> find Tuttle.

                      PROF. WILSON
          I'm doing all I can. I've sent for the
          three best investigators in the city.
          They're our last hope.

BUT UNLESS WE SECURE THE MUMMY OF KING RUTENTUTEN, OUR ENTIRE COLLECTION IS WORTHLESS! WE MUST FIND TUTTLE!

I'M DOING ALL I CAN! I'VE SENT FOR THE THREE BEST INVESTIGATORS IN THE CITY! THEY'RE OUR LAST HOPE!

3 CONTINUED:

At this point we hear a staccato RAP at the door. They
all look off scene. CAMERA SWIPES TO:

4 MED. SHOT AT DOOR

It opens and three figures enter the room wearing peaked
detective caps with bearded masks underneath. In their
mouths are Calabash pipes. They stalk forward about four
steps and come to a halt in front of the three men.

5 CLOSE SHOT - GROUP

The three figures come to attention.

                         FIGURES (in chorus)
              At your service night and day,
              If we don't get 'em you don't pay.
              EXCELSIOR!!!

They wheel around in a goofy salute, revealing they are the
THREE STOOGES, who have walked in backwards, their coats the
same in back as in front, with lapels, buttons, etc., another
set of Calabash pipes in their mouths.

6 CLOSEUP LARRY

He salutes.   LARRY
              Sherlock bones!

PAN TO CURLY   CURLY (salutes)
              Philo Pants!

PAN TO MOE.   MOE (salutes)
              Charlie Chin!

SCENE 5 CONT: STOOGES (in chorus)
              Super sleuths!

                         MOE (to Wilson)
              Where's Professor Tuttle?

                         PROF. WILSON (taken aback)
              He's been kidnapped! That's why we
              sent for you.

                         MOE
              Kidnapped, eh? What did the old boy
              look like?

                         LARRY
              Where was he born?

                         CURLY
              And why?

Moe menaces Curly, who waves goofily.

THIS IS PROFESSOR TUTTLE, GENTLEMEN! YOU MUST FIND HIM!

DON'T WORRY, WE ALWAYS BRING 'EM BACK ALIVE!

EVEN IF THEY'RE DEAD!

5   CONTINUED:

                              CURLY (professionally)
              I withdraw the question.

The professor hands Moe a picture of Prof. Tuttle.
Larry and Curly crowd around to look at it.

7   INSERT - PICTURE,

    showing an old guy with mutton-chop whiskers and horn-
    rimmed glasses as the professor's voice comes over scene.

                         PROF. WILSON'S VOICE
              This is Professor Tuttle, gentlemen.
              You must find him.

8   MED. SHOT

    Moe passes the picture to Curly.

                              CURLY
              Hmm! A walrus!

    Moe bops him, grabs the picture from Curly, turns to the
    professor.

                              MOE
              Don't worry, gentlemen. We always
              brin 'em back alive.

                              CURLY
              Even if they're dead.

                              MOE
              Quiet! dead end!
                 (turns to the boys)
              Get busy. I want you boys to go over the
              ground with a fine toothcomb.

    The Stooges start searching for clues. Moe pulls out a
    magnifying glass, going over the ground in a professional
    manner as Larry gets on his knees and sniffs the floor like
    a bloodhound.

9   CLOSE SHOT - LARRY
                              LARRY
              I got it -- I got a cent!

                         MOE (enters)
              Is it a fresh one?

                         LARRY (displaying a penny)
              1921 Lincoln head.

    Moe grabs Larry's nose and hits his fist on the hand hold-
    ing the nose. Larry squawks and exits as Curly crawls in
    on his hands and knees.

Most of page #4 did not appear in the film; both the gag with Curly scraping the carpet with a comb so he can use the line of dialogue, "I'm going over it with a fine tooth comb," and a rather dragged-out routine to get the Stooges into the basement of the museum were deleted from the film. On screen they

10   MED. CLOSE SHOT

    Curly is on the floor scraping the carpet with a comb as Moe comes down into scene.

                  MOE
        What do you think you're doing?

                  CURLY
        You told me to go over the ground with
        a fine toothcomb.

    Moe burns and grabs the comb away, then pulls the teeth across Curly's head with a LOUD RATCHET effect as Curly yells.

11   MED. SHOT

    (Taking in the Stooges and the two curators.) As Moe and Curly stand up Larry comes into scene.

                  MOE
        Come on, dimwits. We gotta get to
        the bottom of things.

                  CURLY
        Good. We'll start in the basement.

                  LARRY
        The basement!

    The Stooges look around as the professor points to a door on the opposite side of the room.

                  PROF. WILSON
        That's the basement.

    The Stooges rush over to the door. (Gag on exit)

12   MED. CLOSE SHOT - AT DOOR

    The Stooges rush in and Moe and Larry yank vigorously at the door knob trying to pull it open. As they tug away Curly steps in between them and silently pushes them aside. As they look on wonderingly he very easily opens the door by pushing it in the other direction. Moe burns then orders them forward. The three boys step through the door and disappear. As CAMERA HOLDS ON SCENE we hear loud yells accompanied by THUMPS and then a terrific CRASH. The professor and two curators hastily come into scene and look down.

                  PROF. WILSON (yelling o.s.)
        Are you hurt?

                        CUT TO:

just race off screen. There are screams and thuds as they land in the basement while the shocked Professors look down through an open doorway. A cheat! But par for the course in a Stooges comedy.

This 8 × 10 promotional still was not a scene in *We Want Our Mummy*. The Stooges were just cutting up on the set and the still photographer grabbed his camera and clicked. It is not one of the better stills, as the humor seems a bit forced.

13 INT. BASEMENT - MED. CLOSE SHOT

(At the foot of some very steep stairs.) This is a gloomy
room with dim lighting. The Stooges have landed in a heap.

                    MOE
            No! The cement broke our fall.

They get up and as Moe turns to dust himself off he sees
something off scene and reacts, then calls Curly's and
Larry's attention to it.

14 CLOSE SHOT - CORNER OF BASEMENT

A tall, dark, sinister-looking man, Jackson, is clamping
down the lid of a six-foot oblong box. He finishes and
straightens up then turns as the Stooges enter the scene
and confront him. He reacts to the boys' goofy makeup.

                    MOE
            Excuse us for butting in, Mister --
            but we're looking for a professor
            that's been kidnapped. We're detectives.

                    JACKSON (as he looks them over)
            Detectives, eh? Are you coming or going?

                    CURLY
            We're going forward - so that we look
            like we're going backward. Then when
            we go backward we look like we're going
            forward.

                    JACKSON (humoring him)
            And you're looking for a kidnapped
            professor! Well, well!

                    CURLY
            Yeah. He's a horse-faced old guy
            with mutton chops -- looks like a
            comic valentine.

15 INT. OBLONG BOX - CLOSE SHOT PROF. TUTTLE

(The man in the photograph, bound and gagged) He reacts to
Curly's remark in impotent rage. He tries to voice a pro-
test and we hear muffled grunts.

16 INT. BASEMENT - MED. CLOSE SHOT STOOGES AND JACKSON

The boys hear the grunts and look at Jackson suspiciously.
Jackson covers up by pretending to be making a noise.

                    MOE (to Jackson)
            Say, buddy, you oughta take bicarbonate
            of soda.

16 CONTINUED:

                    LARRY
          You haven't seen any suspicious
          characters around here, have you?

                    JACKSON (disarmingly)
          Why no. I'm a new man here and I've
          been very busy packing up this stuff
          to take to the warehouse.
                    (he looks down at the box
                     and continues:)
          Help me carry this out, will you?

                    MOE
          Sure, Mister. You might do us a
          favor some day...I'll take one end --
          Larry, you take the other end and
          Curly, you get in the middle.

17   MED. SHOT

      As Jackson goes over to the door and opens it the three
      Stooges lift the box which is quite heavy. Moe and Larry
      at either end, deposit the box on Curly's shoulders, then
      walk out from under it leaving Curly to support the heavy
      burden alone. He staggers forward with the box on his back.
      He temporarily loses his balance and swings around catching
      Moe on the side of the head. Moe angrily shoves the box
      away from him and it swings around, conking Larry. Curly,
      groaning and complaining, staggers through the open doorway.

18   CLOSE SHOT - CURLY

      Foregoing action.

19   CLOSE SHOT - MOE

      Foregoing action.

20   CLOSE SHOT - LARRY

      Foregoing action.

21   EXT. ALLEY - MED. FULL SHOT

A light truck is parked near the back door of the museum.
A tough-looking driver is at the wheel. The door opens
and Curly staggers out with the box on his shoulders, Moe
and Larry behind him, balancing it. Jackson follows.
Curly stumbles over to the door of the truck and Moe and
Larry topple it off his back into the truck where it lands
with a resounding CRASH.

22   INT. OBLONG BOX - CLOSEUP PROF. TUTTLE

as he is knocked about unmercifully.

23   EXT. ALLEY - MED. SHOT

Curly is still bent over, unable to straighten up. The
driver starts the engine and Jackson climbs into the seat
beside him.

                    JACKSON
          Thanks a million, boys. I'll never
          forget you.

The car starts forward.

                    LARRY
          Gee - he's a nice guy.

24   MED. CLOSE SHOT

Curly, still bent over, whimpers for Moe to help him and
points to his back. Moe burns then kicks Curly in the
pants. We hear a loud noise like the popping of a cork
and Curly straightens up.

                    CURLY (joyfully)
          Thanks, pal.

                    MOE (turns to boys)
          Come on - we've got work to do.

                    CURLY (belligerently)
          Don't try to rush me -- I'll go when
          I'm good and ready.

                    MOE (menacingly)
          Are you ready?

                    CURLY (very meekly)
          Yah, I'm ready.

146

This publicity still has nothing to do with the
story, and also proves that not only Harpo can
play the harp.

Moe grabs Curly by the nose and
the sound effects man gives out
with a "honking" duck call.

Moe raises his arm about to belt
Curly.

Moe's arm on its downward swing
about to let poor Curly have it
again.

147

24 CONTINUED:

They rush back into the building.

CUT TO:

25 INT. EGYPTIAN ROOM - MED. SHOT

Prof. Wilson is bent over opening a vault which is in one
corner of the room. The three Stooges come running into
the room then stop short in the entrance way and react.

26 CLOSE SHOT - STOOGES

Moe points to the professor.

MOE (whispering)
Look! We've caught him redhanded --

CURLY
He's not only a kidsnapper -- he's
also a safe-cracker.

He reaches into his back pocket and pulls out a pair of
handcuffs and the three boys tiptoe forward.

27 MED. SHOT

The boys leap upon the professor, Curly snapping on the
handcuffs. The professor is subdued as Moe starts giving
him the third degree.

MOE (rapid fire)
Caught with the goods, eh? Where's
the professor?

LARRY
Where were you on the night of January
first?

MOE (turns to Curly)
Where were you?

CURLY
Under the table. It was New Year's Eve.

Moe gives Curly a slap. The professor is going wild trying
to get a word in.

28   <u>CLOSE SHOT - PROF. WILSON</u>,

gasping and choking. He manages to find his voice.

                      PROF. WILSON
          What's the meaning of this outrage?
          Take off these handcuffs. You fools,
          I'm Professor Wilson.

29   <u>GROUP SHOT</u>

The boys are taken aback. They look at each other. Curly
unlocks the handcuffs and tries to pass it off.

                    CURLY (in amazement)
          I wondered where I had seen you before.

                    MOE
          Sorry, pal, but we suspect everybody!
          We even suspect each other.
             (he looks at Larry and Curly, who
              nod, then turns back to professor)
          ...And you've got a sneaky look about you.

30   <u>MED. SHOT - GROUP</u>

As the boys dust off the professor and try to pacify him,
Crowl comes into scene. The professor impatiently brushes
the boys aside and turns to Crowl.

                    CROWL
          Have you found any trace of Professor
          Tuttle?

                    PROF. WILSON (angrily)
          No!

                    CROWL
          That means we'll never find the
          missing king.

31   <u>CLOSE SHOT - STOOGES</u>

They prick up their ears as they overhear the remark. Curly
reaches into his pocket and pulls out a playing card.

                    CURLY
          How did they know the king was missing?

Moe and Larry react.

31 CONTINUED:

> MOE (snarling)
> Oh, so it was you, eh? No wonder I
> lost that thirteen cents.

He thumps Curly in the stomach as Larry bangs him in the nose.

32 MED. GROUP SHOT

> PROF. WILSON
> No, no, gentlemen. You don't under-
> stand. The missing king is Rutentuten,
> the third, of Egypt.

> MOE
> Oh! Missing persons are right up
> our alley. When was he last seen?

> PROF. WILSON
> About two thousand years ago.

> MOE
> (breezily)
> A mere bagatelle. Give us two thousand
> years and we'll bring him back.

> CURLY
> Alive.

He quickly ducks from an imaginary blow. The professor
who is fuming, starts to remonstrate, then reconsiders
and draws Crowl aside.

33 CLOSE GROUP SHOT - PROFESSOR AND CROWL

> WILSON (whispering - sotto voce)
> We've got to accept their offer. Nobody
> in his right mind would undertake that
> expedition. It's certain death.

> CROWL (sotto voce)
> Let's hire them before they find out
> about the curse of King Retentuten.

> PROF. WILSON (sotto voce)
> (thinks a moment, then nods)
> Done. And if the curse strikes them
> it will be a blessing to humanity.

Prof. Wilson turns to the boys.

34 <u>GROUP SHOT - STOOGES AND PROFESSORS</u>

           PROF. WILSON
      Gentlemen, you're hired. We're sending
      you to bring back the mummy of King
      Rutentuten. You will leave immediately
      for Cairo.

           CURLY
  Hmm!
        (he turns to Moe and Larry)
      I got an uncle who lives in Cairo --
      he's a Cairo-practor. Knk! Knk! Knk!

He wags his head cockily as Moe belts him one.

           PROF. WILSON (to the boys)
      If you succeed we will pay you five
      thousand dollars.

The Stooges nod then react as Crowl speaks.

           CROWL
      The recovery of the mummy will prove
      of untold value to science.

           MOE (dramatically)
  To science!

           LARRY (striking a pose)
  To science!

           CURLY
      For five thousand bucks!

With this, the Stooges rush over to the three men, do the
"Viva la France" gag, quickly kiss them on each cheek,
then turn to kiss each other and bump heads. They dash
about madly, crying:

           STOOGES
      Egype, here we come!
      Viva la science, etc.

The professors look on in amazement as the Stooges rush
out the door.

                    WIPE TO:

In script page #11 the Stooges are just supposed to kiss the professors on each cheek but Curly adds a little something extra. He grabs one of the professors and wraps his arms around him. Ad libbing as he goes, he sweeps him off his feet and plants a kiss on his cheek. When he realizes what he's doing, he lets go and the professor goes crashing to the floor.

The cab driver, played by character actor Eddie Laughton, was originally the Stooges straight man in vaudeville. The script actually called for the cab driver to be "a little meek type." That certainly was not Eddie Laughton. My guess is that my father suggested him for the part in the film and as the cab driver's demeanor was not important to the role, he got the part.

35   EXT. STREET - MED. FULL SHOT

A taxicab is parked at the curb. The driver, Jake, is a
little, meek type. A sign on the back of the cab reads:

"BRONX TAXICAB CO"

The three Stooges are piling into the cab. Moe pauses
for an instant as the driver turns to him.

DRIVER
Where to?

MOE
Egypt.

The driver nods his head then suddenly does a big belated
take. He shrugs his shoulders then reaches over and
pushes down the taximeter flag.

36   INSERT - METER

Hand pulling down the meter handle as "15¢" is
registered.

LAP DISSOLVE TO:

37   INSERT - METER (TRAVELING)

The meter now reads, "$2,198.55"

LAP DISSOLVE TO:

The taxi meters in the cab sequence, in the vernacular of the motion picture business, are called "inserts." Inserts are shot on a special stage with a short crew after all the scenes in the script are completed. A great deal of money was saved by the studio not having a full crew and actors waiting for this close-up of a taxi meter to be shot.

If one looks carefully at this photograph of the cab, seeming to bake in the hot sun of the Egyptian desert, one can see the poorly executed cyclorama (canvas backdrop) with sand bags stuffed into the corner at the far right to hold down the edges of the canvas.

I'm sure that everyone will be able to recognize Moe's voice in the commercial that comes over the cab's radio. Jules White, in order to save money would have my father or one of the other Stooges do voice-overs whenever possible.

13

38   EXT. DESERT SET #1 - MED. SHOT CAB (PAN SHOT)

Jake, the driver, still at the wheel and the three Stooges
in the back seat. The cab is bumping along, the tires all
flat and chewed to ribbons. The fenders are loose and flap
in the breeze like chicken wings.

39   INT. CAB - MED. CLOSE SHOT

One of the jump seats is pulled out and the top of it is being used as a table on which are some dishes. On another
seat rests a portable stove where Curly is cooking dinner.
Oriental music is heard from a portable radio. Moe is peering out the window thru a spy glass while Larry is peeling
potatoes and helping Curly fix dinner. The music suddenly
stops and the voice of the announcer is heard.
(NOTE: Curly wears coveralls, cut off at the knee, a
         zipper runs the full lenth of the front. All
         wear pith helmets.)

                    VOICE
          You have been listening to Ali
          Ben Woodman and his Swinging Bed-
          ouins... Do you need money? Bor-
          row on your camel or elephant.
          Oasis Loan Company provides quick,
          confidential service -- no red
          tape, no co-signers....

Moe angrily snaps off the radio.

                    LARRY
          Wherever you go - commercial an-
          nouncements. /If we don't get to
          a filling station pretty soon,
          I'll die of thirst.

                    MOE
          Me, too -- I'm so dry my tongue
          feels like a bale of hay.

Moe brings the telescope up to his eye and looks around. As
he brings the telescope around it stops right in front of
Larry's hair.

40   INSERT - LARRY'S HAIR

(Shooting thru telescope mat.)

CONTINUATION SCENE 39:
Moe gazes for a few seconds into instrument.

This photograph has always been a popular
one and has been used for lobby cards and one-
sheets.

40 CONTINUED

>   MOE
>   (exclaims excitedly)
>   We're coming to a jungle! I can
>   see the tangled underbrush! Cam-
>   els are walking thru it!

He looks up, realizes what he has been looking at, reacts,
then bops Larry on the head with telescope. He turns to
driver.

>   MOE
>   Stop the cab! We gotta find water.

Off scene we hear a loud SCREECH of brakes. The Stooges
land in a heap of dishes and suitcases.

41 EXT. CAB - MED. SHOT - DESERT SET #1 (Redressed

There is no top on the cab. Suddenly from the top a big
ship's anchor is tossed out by Curly. This is followed by
a Jacob's ladder which unrolls over the side of the cab.
The three boys come out and clamber down the ladder, step-
ping on each other's heads and hands.

42 MED. CLOSE SHOT

The boys look around.

>   MOE
>   Now, we're in for it. Lost on the
>   desert and no water.

>   LARRY
>   (looks off and reacts)
>   Look! There's a signpost! Maybe
>   we ain't so lost.

43 MED. CLOSE SHOT OF SIGNPOST

reading: "CAIRO CITY LIMITS". A few pieces of ruins are visible. Underneath sign are four arrows pointing in different
directions, each marked: "TUNIS 1500 MILES". The Stooges come
into scene and stare at the signs.

>   MOE
>   Oh, boy, we're nearly in Cairo. The
>   tomb oughta be around here some place.

>   CURLY
>   I'd rather go to Tunis. Then we
>   could have Tunis sandwiches for lunch.

43 CONTINUED:

    Moe goes to bop Curly, who ducks. Curly looks off and re-
    acts.

                CURLY
        Look -- water!

44 LONG SHOT MIRAGE OF OCEAN ON SAND (COMPOSITE SHOT)

    A large ship is visible.

45 MED. SHOT

                CURLY
        Oh, boy -- the ocean. We can take
        a bath.

    Moe and Larry look off in the indicated direction.

46 LONG SHOT DESERT

    showing a long stretch of sand.

47 CLOSE GROUP SHOT

                MOE
        (turns away disgustedly)
      Ocean nothing! That's a mirage.

                CURLY
      Go on, you can't fool me. A mirage
      is what you keep your automobile in...
        (Moe burns and glares)
      That's the ocean. I'm going swimming!
        (he runs from scene)

48 MED. SHOT DESERT

    Curly runs in, daintily pulls up his pants as though going
    wading and runs forward. He sticks one toe in imaginary
    water then runs back as if a wave were coming. Then he wades
    in. He splashes himself like a baby in the surf, dunking
    his seater and shivering.

The sequence with Curly putting his toe into a hot, desert-sand mirage and making you swear that it was the ice-cold ocean after watching him shriek and shiver, demonstrates his incredible versatility in the use of facial expressions and body motions.

48A   <u>CLOSEUP MOE AND LARRY</u>

      look on in wide-eyed amazement.

48B   CONTINUED:
      Curly lies on his stomach and swims on the sand. He gets up
      and comes back toward the boys.

49   CONTINUED:
      Larry and Moe are flabbergasted as Curly comes running to
      them.

                    CURLY
            Gee, the water's wonderful!

                    MOE
            Water!
               (looks at Larry)
            Say, maybe he's got something there.

                    CURLY
            You think I'm crazy. Come on, try
            it. It's nice and cold.

      The three boys start taking off their coats.

                    MOE
            The only way to hit cold water is to
            dive in quick and get it over with.

                    CURLY
            Come on, fellers. Last one in is
            an old-maid.

      Woo-wooing, he runs up on a huge sand dune by Moe and Larry.

50   <u>MED. SHOT AT SAND DUNE</u>

      The boys poise for an instant and then dive off head first.
      They hit the ground and go right through, disappearing from
      sight. HOLD ON SCENE as long, drawn-out wails come over,
      followed by three HOLLOW THUMPS.

51   <u>INT. TOMB (PASSAGEWAY) - MED. SHOT</u>

      The three Stooges are sprawled in a heap on the floor of a
      dark passageway. Several stone blocks in the wall are cov-
      ered with Egyptian hieroglyphics. In b.g. are a few statues
      of Egyptian gods. On each side of the statues are blazing
      oil torches. The boys pick themselves up and look around.

17

51 CONTINUED:

                         MOE
              I wonder where we are!

                         LARRY
              Maybe we're in the subway.

Curly suddenly notices the hieroglyphics and points at them.

                         CURLY
              Look! Animals! Why we're in the
              zoo.

Moe gives him a slap.

                         MOE (scornfully)
              Animals! You idiot! That's Egyp-
              tian writing.

                         LARRY
              What does it say?

52   CLOSE SHOT AT WALL (TAKING IN STOOGES)

       A small panel in the wall behind them opens and two evil eyes
       peer out.

                         VOICE (ominously)
              This is the tomb of the mighty King
              Rutentuten!

       The boys react to the voice. Moe turns to Curly, thinking
       he has spoken.

                         MOE
              I didn't know you could read Egyp-
              tian.

                         CURLY
              That didn't come out of me.

                         VOICE (continuing)
              Infidels! Prepare to die!

53   MED. SHOT STOOGES

       As they hear this they react in a panic, and start running
       around wildly, bumping into each other, until finally Moe
       stops and grabs Curly and Larry.

53 CONTINUED:

MOE
Get a grip on yourselves. There's
nothing to be scared of. Come on,
let's get out of here.

The boys remove torches from the wall and start forward
fearfully,. CAMERA TRUCKING with them. A knife comes sailing right past Moe's nose and buries itself in the wall.

54   DIFFERENT ANGLE

The Stooges react, turn and start out in the opposite direction when a skeleton quickly drops down from the ceiling and
dangles in front of Curly. He lets out a yell, turns and
bumps into Larry and Moe, bowling them over. They scramble
to their feet, turn and run.

55   MED. CLOSE TRUCK SHOT ANOTHER SPOT

The three Stooges move on, holding their torches aloft. As
they cautiously creep forward, a long, bony arm comes out of
the darkness, grabs Larry around the mouth and yanks him out
of scene, unnoticed by Moe and Curly. Curly and Moe continue
to prowl forward as the arm comes out again, grabs Moe by
the mouth and drags him out of scene, unnoticed by Curly.

56   CLOSE SHOT CURLY

He continues to move forward apprehensively.

CURLY (nervously)
Gee, fellers, it's spooky in here.
If you weren't right behind me, I'd
be scared stiff.

The bony arm comes out to grab Curly, but at this instant
Curly bends over to examine a wall and the arm misses him.
Curly straightens up.

CURLY
There oughta be a door --
(turns around and sees
the outstretched arm)
This hall has gotta end somewhere...

Suddenly he does a double take, slaps the hand away, barks at
it, turns and runs out of scene.

57   INT. SMALL CELL - MED. CLOSE SHOT

There are bars in front and in the back are some draperies
which hang down to about three feet from the ground. Moe and
Larry are in the cell staring upward at the draperies. Behind the drapes we see a foot pedaling an emery wheel and two
hands with a large scimitar which is being sharpened. Moe
and Larry react, look at each other and feel their throats.
They gulp nervously. Moe looks down, sees several large rocks
on the ground. He points to them and Larry nods. They reach
down and each picks up a rock. They wind up and fling them
toward the draperies. From behind the drapes we hear a LOUD
GRUNT of pain. Moe and Larry turn and run out of the cell.

58   CLOSEUP

foregoing action.

59   ANOTHER SPOT IN PASSAGEWAY - CLOSE SHOT CURLY

He comes in calling for Moe and Larry, then cups his hands
and shouts loudly.

                    CURLY
          Where are you?

                    ECHO
          Where are you?

                    CURLY (reacts and smiles)
          Hmm! An echo. Knk! Knk! Knk!
               (now acts playful)
          I'm here. Where are you?

                    ECHO
          I'm here. Where are you?

                    CURLY
          I asked you first. Where are you?

                    ECHO
          None of your business.

                    CURLY (chuckles)
          Knk knk knk!
               (suddenly he does a big
                delayed take, then screams)
          Help! The place is haunted!

He starts running around wildly, pawing his face, then turns
to the wall and starts pounding on it trying to find a way out

Curly does his familiar face wipes
as he reacts in fear to an echo
which gets a bit too friendly.

60   INSERT   SMALL JUTTING PEG

Curly's hand bangs against the peg, pushing it in.

CONTINUATION SCENE 59:
Slowly a rock door raises, making a good-sized entrance way.
Curly reacts to this and dashes in. The door slowly closes
behind him.

61   INT. CHAMBER   MED. SHOT

This room contains a number of relics, pottery, etc., also a
female mummy standing upright. On the other side of the room
is a male mummy, standing upright in an open sarcophagus.
Curly is on. He looks around, sees the female mummy which
has its back to him, and goes over to it.

62   CLOSE SHOT   MUMMY AND CURLY

Curly taps the mummy on the shoulder.

                    CURLY
          Pardon me -- would you please tell
          me how to get out of here?
               (waits for reply but
                none is forthcoming)
          What's the matter -- cat got your
          tongue?

Curly shakes it a minute, then looks around into the female
mummy's face and reacts.

                    CURLY
          Oh, excuse me, lady -- I didn't know
          you're a mummy!

He tips his hat at it, looks off, sees the other mummy and
rushes over to it.

63   CLOSE SHOT   AT SARCOPHAGUS

Curly comes into scene and stares at the mummy. He gets excited.

                    CURLY
          Hmm! You must be Rutentuten!
               (rubs his hands)
          I found him! King, old kid, you're
          going on a trip.

63   CONTINUED:

                          MUMMY (in sepulchral tones)
              That's what you think!

                          CURLY
              Well, them's my orders --

Suddenly he does a big take and lets out a scream.

64   MED. SHOT

     Curly backs away, frightened, as the mummy, which is a phony,
     steps out of the sarcophagus with arms outstretched. Curly
     falls backward over a small object. The mummy reaches down
     to grab him and as Curly tries to scramble out of his reach,
     the mummy leaps over him. Curly, cornered and trying to get
     away, leaps over the mummy and lands on all fours. The mummy
     leaps over Curly's back, landing in a crouching position.
     They play leap frog like this across the room until Curly,
     leaping over the mummy's shoulders, crashes into the wall.

65   CLOSE SHOT   CURLY AND MUMMY

     Curly's hand closes on a bludgeon and as he scrambles to his
     feet, he gives the mummy two in the eyes. The mummy lets out
     a grunt, holds its eyes and backs out of scene. Curly, still
     holding the bludgeon, looks around for an instant, then
     dashes over to the spot where the door was and frantically
     tries to find it.

66   CLOSE SHOT AT WALL

     Curly, frightened out of his wits, wheels around looking back
     toward the mummy, at the same time backing up. His fanny
     bumps against the jutting peg, causing the door to raise
     slowly.

67   INSERT: THE PEG
     catches Curly's belt and starts to lift him.

68   MED. LONG SHOT

     The peg lifts Curly into the air. He is suspended just above
     the opening, his hand still clutching the bludgeon. As he
     struggles to free himself -

When Moe belts Curly in the stomach, Curly's leg shoots out in a reflex action and catches Moe under the chin. I found a frame which looks a bit too real for comfort—for Moe's comfort that is.

165

69   INT. PASSAGEWAY MED. CLOSE SHOT AT OPENING

Moe and Larry come running into scene, looking around for
Curly. They see the opening and immediately start through it.

70   INT. CHAMBER MED. SHOT

As Moe and Larry come thru the opening, Curly looks down,
sees their heads appear. He lets out a yell of fright and
brings the bludgeon down on their heads. They tumble forward
into the room and sit up groggily as Curly recognizes them
and realizes his mistake.

                    CURLY (apologetically)
          Gee, I'm sorry. I thought you guys
          were the mummy!

Moe burns, gets to his feet and belts Curly in the stomach.
Curly grunts and automatically raises his foot, catching Moe
under the chin, knocking him backwards to the floor. Larry
grabs Curly and pulls him down.

71   MED. SHOT

Curly crashes to the floor and quickly scrambles to his feet.
Behind him the door slowly closes. Curly turns to Moe and
Larry.

                    CURLY (excitedly)
          Hey, fellers - did you ever hear a
          mummy talking?
               (Moe and Larry shake their
               heads)
               (Curly sings)
          Well, I did.

Moe and Larry nod, then take it and look at each other.

                    LARRY (to Moe)
          Now, he's talking to mummies. Next
          thing you know, he'll be telling us
          he played games with it.

                    CURLY
          Soitanly! Leap frog. He was right
          here a minute ago.

He walks out of scene, Larry following him, leaving Moe there.

A publicity still which proves the following equation: 1 part Curly + one part ugly mummy = photographic phun.

72   CLOSEUP MOE

He reacts in disgust.

                    MOE (sneering)
          Who ever heard of a mummy walking
          and talking! What nonsense!

While he is saying this, the mummy's arm comes into scene behind him, the hand resting on his shoulder. Moe reacts nervously. Afraid to look around, he calls out.

                    MOE
          Hey, one of you guys get your hand
          off my shoulder.

73   CLOSE SHOT CURLY AND LARRY

(In another part of the room)

                    CURLY
          How can we touch you way over here!

He and Larry turn toward Moe and react.

74   CLOSE SHOT MOE AND MUMMY

Moe, trembling, slowly brings his hand up to his shoulder and
feels the mummy's hand. He reacts, slowly turns his head,
lets out a yell as he looks into the mummy's grotesque face,
and tears out of scene.

75   MED. CLOSE SHOT CURLY AND LARRY

as Moe comes tearing into scene between them, knocking them up
against the wall. The impact opens a secret panel which opens
like a revolving door, catches the boys amidships and propels
them into the next chamber. The panel shuts after them.

76   INT. KING'S CHAMBER - MED. FULL SHOT

This is a lavish tomb containing another more elaborate mummy
on a stone table, wearing a small crown, flanked on either
side by two blazing torches. Near the mummy are statues of
gods, urns, vases, tapestries on the wall, etc. In b.g. we
see a well. Near it is a crude-looking water jug with a rope
attached. The boys come tumbling into the room and sit up
groggily.

Curly's line on Script page #24 "A tisket, a tasket, a green and yellow basket," was from a very popular song of the day.

77   CLOSE GROUP SHOT

Moe looks off, reacts and shouts.

                MOE
        Hey, look! There's King Rutentuten!

The boys get to their feet. Moe and Larry rush over to it.

78   MED. CLOSE SHOT

Moe and Larry run in to the mummy, rubbing their hands joy-
fully.

                MOE
        No mistake about him. He's the
        real McCoy.

                LARRY
        I thought his name was Rutentuten.

Moe is about to crack Larry when we hear a loud woo-wooing
from Curly o.s. Moe and Larry react . Curly excitedly runs
in woo-wooing for all he's worth.

                CURLY
        I found it! I found it!

                MOE
        Found what?

                CURLY
        A tisket, a tasket, a little yellow
        basket.

As he says this, he holds up an Egyptian basket. Moe gives
Curly a belt which sends him reeling out of scene backwards.

79   CLOSE SHOT AT WELL

Curly totters backwards into scene and falls into the well with
a loud yell. Moe and Larry run into scene, Moe carrying a big
blazing torch. They peer down into well as we hear a loud,
drawn-out wail from Curly and then a big wave of water splashes
into scene, drenching Moe and Larry. As they hear cries of
"Help!" from Curly, Moe drops the rope in the hole as he
hands Larry the torch.

80   MED. SHOT

Moe pulls on the rope and hauls Curly to the surface, helps
him out of the well. Curly shakes himself like a dog splashing water all over Moe.

81   <u>CLOSEUP MOE</u>

as the water hits him. He burns.

82   <u>MED. CLOSE SHOT</u>

Moe reaches over, grabs Curly by the ears and twists them.
Two streams of water fly out of his ears. Curly lets out a
yell as Moe addresses the boys.

                  MOE
        Get going, boneheads! We can't stay
        in this tomb all day. Let's move
        the king out of here.

He strides over to the mummy with Larry following him. As
Curly starts out he pauses, turns back with an after-thought.

            CURLY (looking at well)
      Hmm! That's dangerous.

He picks up a heavy rug and carefully covers the hole. He
then dusts his hands in satisfaction and runs after the boys.

83   <u>MED. CLOSE SHOT</u>

The two Stooges are in front of the King's dummy, as Curly
enters.

              MOE (to Larry and Curly)
      Come on, bring the mummy and be care-
      full He's worth five thousand bucks
      to us. I'll go see if I can find
      that door again.

He exits out of scene. Curly goes over to the mummy and bends
over to lift it up.

84   <u>INSERT - BLAZING TORCH</u>

Curly's fanny contacts the blazing torch.

CONTINUATION OF SCENE 83:
Curly lets out a yell and leaps forward, dumping the mummy
and falling on top of it.

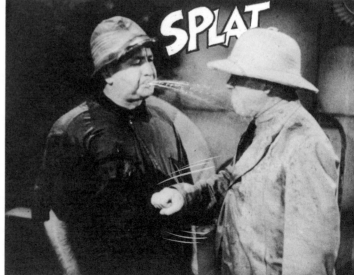

85   CLOSE SHOT CURLY

flat on the mummy. Larry rushes into scene and helps him to
his feet. As he does so, we see the mummy is now nothing but
a lot of empty bandages and a small pile of dust. The boys
stare down at it. Curly reaches down and picks up the bandages.

                    CURLY
          Look! He's unraveled!

Moe comes into scene and takes it as he sees what's left of
the mummy. He gives Curly and Larry the double slap and
bawls them out.

                    MOE
          Dumbbells! You've ruined every-
          thing! Five thousand bucks gone
          with the dust!

As he goes to bat Curly, a scream for help comes over scene
from adjoining chamber. The boys react, run over to the wall
and peer thru a crevice.

86   CLOSE SHOT CREVICE IN WALL

The Stooges peeking through.

87   INT. NEXT CHAMBER - MED. SHOT

Jackson the kidnapper, seen in the first sequence - an evil-
looking Egyptian henchman carrying a scimitar and the phony
mummy are dragging Prof. Tuttle into the room as he calls for
help. They fling him to the floor and look around.

                    JACKSON (taking scimitar)
          Listen, Tuttle, you've been leading
          me all over this tomb for hours to
          give those pals of yours a chance to
          get the mummy. Well, you better
          talk before I say three! Where is
          that mummy!
               (threatens Tuttle with
                Scimitar)
          One -- two -- !

                    TUTTLE (weakly)
          Wait - wait!
               (gulps, points shaking
                finger toward the wall)
          It's in there! I don't know where
          the door is.

87 CONTINUED:

                    JACKSON (turns to henchmen)
          Tear down the wall.

The men grab up picks and shovels and start hacking at the
wall as Jackson turns back to Tuttle menacingly.

                    JACKSON
          You better be telling the truth,
          because if that mummy isn't in there,
          intact, it's the finish for you and
          those three goofs. Get it?

88 INT. CHAMBER - MED. SHOT STOOGES

peering thru the crevice. They react as they hear this, and
back away fearfully.

                    CURLY (very excited)
          Woo! If they find out we killed
          that mummy, they'll kill us. What'll
          we do?

                    MOE (thinks a moment then snaps
                              fingers)
          I got an idea!
              (turns to Curly)
          We'll make a mummy out of you and
          fool 'em.

                    CURLY
          I can't be a mummy -- I'm a daddy.

                    MOE
          All right - so you can be a daddy
          mummy.

                    CURLY
          Oh - that's different.

Moe reaches into his pocket and takes out a small box as
Larry picks up some of the bandages.

89 INSERT OF BOX

showing needles, thread, buttons, etc.

CONTINUATION SCENE 88:

                    MOE
          It's a good thing I'm an old tailor.

                    CURLY
          Pass the bottle - knk knk.

As they start to bandage Curly -

                                        DISSOLVE TO:

90   INT. KING'S CHAMBER - MED. CLOSE SHOT STOOGES

      Curly is now almost completely swathed in bandages with only
      his eyes and nose visible.

                    CURLY (protesting)
          Hey, I can hardly breathe!

                    MOE
          Shut your mouth and breathe thru
          your ears.

      He and Larry station Curly rigidly in the place of the other
      dummy. Over scene we hear the POUNDING and HAMMERING of the
      looters.

      CONTINUATION SCENE 87:
      Jackson and the henchmen are still hacking away furiously at
      the wall. The wall starts to crumble and they pull aside
      enough mortar to make an entrance.

91   INT. KING'S CHAMBER - MED. FULL SHOT

      As Jackson and the henchmen break thru Moe and Larry rush over
      to greet them. The looters pull up in surprise. Prof.
      Tuttle comes up in b.g.

92   MED. SHOT

                    JACKSON (suspiciously)
          So, you guys are in here, eh? Where's
          Rutentuten?

                    MOE (pointing to Curly)
          Right there, and he's as good as new.

      Jackson goes over to Curly as the henchmen, Moe and Larry
      follow.

93   CLOSE GROUP SHOT

The group approach Curly. Jackson bends over and looks at
Curly.

                    JACKSON
          Boy, was he homely!

94   BIG CLOSEUP CURLY

He reacts, then quickly resumes his pose.

CONTINUATION SCENE 93:

                    1ST HENCHMAN
          Say, where's the jewels that are
          supposed to be buried with it?

                    JACKSON
          They always wrap the jewels inside
          the mummy. We got to cut him open.

95   CLOSEUP CURLY

taking this big.

96   CLOSEUP MOE AND LARRY

reacting.

97   MED. CLOSE SHOT

The henchmen lay Curly on the floor as Moe and Larry in b.g.
react fearfully. Jackson turns to his men.

                    JACKSON
          Who's got a sharp knife?

98   CLOSE SHOT CURLY AND MOE

As Curly hears this, he sits up. Moe sees him rise, kicks
him in the face, knocking Curly flat on his back.

99   MED. CLOSE GROUP SHOT

The Egyptian henchman hands Jackson the scimitar.

100   CLOSE SHOT CURLY

As Jackson turns away from Curly, Curly reacts, takes hold of
the zipper and zips it open.

101   GROUP SHOT

Jackson, holding the scimitar turns back to Curly to cut
the bandages. He stops and reacts.

                    JACKSON (exclaiming)
        Look! He burst open and there's a
        zipper on him!
                    (turns suspiciously to group)
        Say, did they have zippers in them days?

                    MOE
        Sure. Don't you know the old Egyptian
        proverb - a zipper a day keeps the
        doctor away.

Jackson gives Moe a look and turns back to Curly. He starts
searching around his chest, feels something.

                    JACKSON
        I've got it! The ruby of Rutentuten!

He pulls out a huge dollar watch, reacts, then looks menacingly at Moe and Larry.

                    JACKSON
        Now, don't tell me they had watches,
        too!

                    MOE
        Why, sure they did. They used them
        to check their sundials.

Jackson reaches into Curly's chest again, pulls out a newspaper. Headline reads: "YANKS WIN WORLD SERIES".

102   INSERT OF NEWSPAPER

103   CLOSEUP JACKSON

Foregoing action. He looks at Curly.

104   BIG CLOSEUP CURLY'S FACE

Foregoing action. Curly opens his eyes trying to peek, sees
Jackson and, realizing he is caught, waves friendly like.

105   MED. SHOT GROUP

Moe and Larry react to this. Jackson turns upon them furiously.

                    JACKSON
          Hi-jackers, eh?!

He throws paper down. Curly jumps up and starts to run, followed by Moe and Larry.

                    JACKSON (to henchmen)
          Get 'em, boys!

Jackson and the henchmen make a lunge for the Stooges who
elude them and run around the room, then over to the other
side where the well is covered with the rug. The looters
pause for an instant then leap toward the Stooges. As they
step on the rug, Jackson and his two henchmen drop out of
sight with loud YELLS. We hear a SPLASH as they hit bottom.
The boys react as Prof. Tuttle comes up to them. (NOTE:
ROUTINE TO BE WORKED OUT.)

106   CLOSEUP STOOGES

Foregoing action.

107   MED. CLOSE SHOT GROUP

                         MOE
          Come on, Professor - let's get out
          of here.

                         LARRY
          But what about King Rutentuten and
          the five grand?

                         CURLY
          The wind blew him away.

                    PROF. TUTTLE
          That wasn't King Rutentuten -- that
          was his wife Queen Hotsi Totsi.

As the boys react to this, the Professor picks up a little
sarcophagus about three feet long.

                    PROF. TUTTLE
          This is Rutentuten -- he was a mid-
          get.

The Stooges react joyously, grab the Professor and run from
the room. (GET GAG EXIT)

108   EXT. ENTRANCE TO TOMB - NEAR SIGN

This is like a mine-shaft opening. The group comes running
out, stop and look off.

                    MOE
      Taxi!

He raises his hand in a taxi signal and all run out.

109   MED. SHOT A SAND DUNE (DESERT BACKGROUND)

The body of the taxi is visible behind the sand dune as the
Stooges rush in and climb in taxi.

110   MED. CLOSE SHOT

As the Stooges get in, Moe hesitates and addresses the
same taxi-driver.

                    MOE
      New York!

                    DRIVER
      New York!
           (honks his horn)

111   LONG SHOT

The taxi moves from behind the sand dune and we see the taxi
body is mounted on an elephant. As it proceeds across the
desert -

                              FADE OUT.

                    THE END

On page #32 another expensive ending bit the dust. Animals, especially elephants, are costly when it comes to filmmaking. The time it would take to mount a taxi body on an elephant, not to speak of the trainer to keep him out of trouble and the bales of hay to keep him nourished, would be far too costly for a Stooges comedy. Although the gag is a cute one, the director, Jules White, must have seen big bucks flying out the window. Consequently, they traded the elephant in for an alligator.

108	MED. SHOT AT HOLE IN WALL

A huge alligator comes slithering through and stops.

109	MED. SHOT - GROUP

They are preparing to leave. Curly turns and sees the alligator.

>   CURLY
>   Look! A mummy alligator! I'm going
>   to take him home.

He exits toward the alligator and starts to look it over.

110	MED. CLOSE SHOT

Curly approaches the alligator and reaches toward it.

>   CURLY
>   This'll look swell on my wall.

111	BIG CLOSEUP - ALLIGATOR

Curly's hand (DOUBLE) strokes the alligator's head. It opens it jaws and snaps at the hand.

111A	CLOSEUP - CURLY

He nearly swallows his tongue, turns and runs.

111B	CLOSEUP - ALLIGATOR

It starts after him.

111C	MED. SHOT - THE GROUP

Curly dashes in yelling. The others look off, see the alligator and run out.

>   FADE OUT:

The alligator solves the problem of the gag exit requested by the writer in the last line on script page #31. It suffices to have the Stooges doing their typical dash off screen as they FADE OUT in the first, revised ending. The actual ending which appears in the film goes the revised script ending one better. In the final frame we have the Stooges running off into the desert sunset toward their taxi, with Curly "woo wooing" as the film FADES OUT.

YES, WE HAVE NO BONANZA

About the Film

Yes, We Have No Bonanza (Prod. No. 438) was the Stooges' 39th film and was released in 1939. The title was obviously a play on words on the title of a famous song of the day, "Yes, We Have No Bananas." Although the film essentially follows the script, the opening scenes were slightly different. The script starts with the camera moving in on Curly, who appears to be on horseback. When the camera PULLS BACK he is on a strange bicycle which bounces up and down like a pogo stick. In contrast, the actual film opens on a saloon called "Maxey's Place," which is another example of how things change when the celluloid winds up in the hands of the film editor.

It is interesting to note that a lake set had been built on Columbia's Stage 6 for the Stooges' previous short, *A Ducking They Did Go*. Ever mindful of the meager budgets on a Stooges comedy, the producers used this same set, with a bit of added set dressing, for the mining sequence in *Bonanza*.

As I explained previously in Lucien Ballard's biography, Leonard Maltin (in his book *The Art of the Cinematographer*), asked Ballard a question regarding Stooges comedies and camera trickery. In reply, Ballard explained, "Everything was done on the set." The scene Ballard was probably referring to when he spoke of explosions being created with flash powder placed in a trough underneath the camera was undoubtedly a scene similar to the last sequence in *Yes, We Have No Bonanza*, where the crook's car crashes through the wall of the jail. After the crash they CUT—then the flash powder was ignited under the camera and when the smoke cleared it revealed the car inside the Sheriff's office with the set redressed and added debris scattered everywhere. The illusion on screen is: CRASH! EXPLOSION! RESULT! and the effect, though crude, works every time.

Another type of special effect found in *Bonanza* was the process screen, which was utilized in two scenes: one where the crooks drive off in their car with the stolen money and the other with the Stooges following on the fake horse's back with Curly holding on to the horse's tail for dear life.

This simple process screen, a far cry from the computerized methods of the eighties, was filmed in the following manner back in the thirties and is still in use today although it has been improved upon.

In the scene with the heavy's car, the first thing that had to be done was to mount the camera on a camera car which then drove down a Western street, filming the required background for the scene. Now, we have a film which was shot from a moving car with the scenery flying by. The developed film was then brought to the process stage and projected onto a rear projection screen. Then the car was placed in front of the screen on a vibrating platform to simulate motion and, of course, the driver simulated turning the wheel, to give the illusion that he was driving. With the moving images on the process screen speeding by in the background, the illusion in the final print was the car driving through the countryside.

Watching he final effect on the movie screen one would swear the car was speeding along an actual road, even though it was really standing still. This type of "process" scene can be filmed through side, rear or front windows of the car, depending on the angle chosen by the director. The same type of process screen, with a different background film in the projector, was used in the scene with Curly (obviously supported by wires) being pulled along holding the fake horse's tail. In the frame I chose, one can see the blurred images of buildings in an old western town which was part of Columbia's back lot in Burbank, known as the Columbia Ranch.

The Stooges rarely used doubles, but they were a must in *Yes, We Have No Bonanza*. The sequence with the Stooges jumping off the roof onto the horse's back was a stunt they were not capable of doing and called for experienced stunt men to double for the Stooges. The action moves so fast in the actual film that only by slowing down the individual frames on an editing machine are you aware that these men are not the Three Stooges. At one point a dummy is used—and not a very good one at that. In many instances where dummies were employed in Stooges shorts, they were so obvious that they received unexpected howls of laughter. And in a Stooges comedy, since the object was to get laughs, planned or unplanned, no one complained.

Yes, We Have No Bonanza was not the best of Stooges comedies nor was it worst. There was plenty of slapstick fun and I enjoyed hearing the Stooges sing harmony (a favorite pastime of my father). The beer mug tossing by Curly piqued my curiousity. As I pored over the film frames I was still mystified as to how Curly tossed the beer right into Moe's outstretched hand. I was certain that the glass must have come in on a wire, but I searched every frame for it and was unable to find a thing. In all probability, the wired glass must have started out in Moe's hand and been yanked into Curly's after which he performed a reverse throwing motion. Then, when the finished film was reversed, it would look as though Curly threw the glass and Moe miraculously caught it. I am happy to say that one of the many enjoyable aspects of preparing these script books has been the opportunity to study the scenes frame-by-frame in an attempt to solve the mysteries of the vast assortment of camera and special effects trickery that were used in the Stooges comedies.

The Stars

Larry

Moe

Curly

The Cast

182

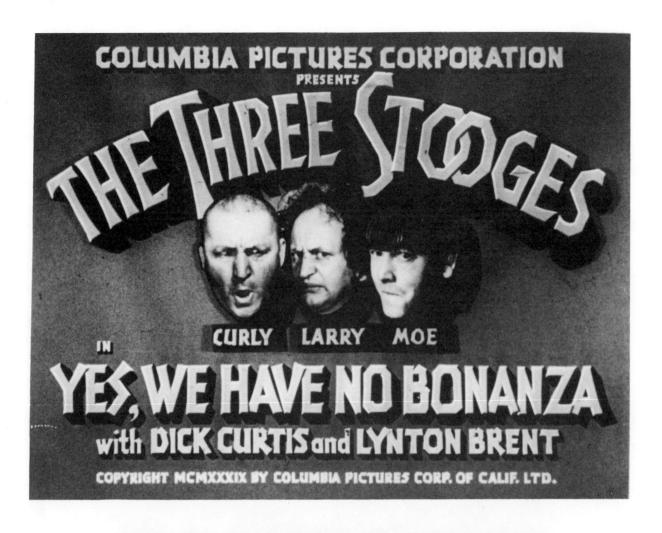

"YES WE HAVE NO BONANZAS"

STOOGE #5 - PROD.#438

By

Searle Kramer
Elwood Ullman

FINAL DRAFT CONTINUITY
NOVEMBER 10, 1938

PRODUCER - JULES WHITE
DIRECTOR - DEL LORD

I don't know why, but the title on the script cover was *Yes, We Have No Bonanzas* (plural) while on the screen it is in the singular. Another discrepancy from script to film is Jules White's credit. On the script cover he is the Producer but on screen he is listed as the Associate Producer.

184

STOOGE #5 - PRODUCTION #438

FADE IN: (DAY)

1   EXT. WESTERN STREET - TRAVELING SHOT - WAIST FIGURE OF CURLY

He is riding along at a jaunty pace, evidently on a horse.
His ten-gallon hat and bandana wave in the breeze. PULL
CAMERA BACK disclosing Curly on one of those new type bicycles
-- (INGO BIKES). Off center traction which makes Curly bump
like he is galloping. Curly is dressed in an old suit. He
wears boots and spurs in addition to the bandana and cowboy
hat. CAMERA PANS WITH HIM as he rides up to the front of
the "ALKALI CITY SALOON". He stops the bike and leans it
against a hitching post, then taking a weight like that used
to hold harness horses from the basket on the handlebars, he
drops it on the ground as if he were leaving his horse.

                CURLY
        Don't go away, Old Silver.

He pats the handlebars as if they were a horse and very bow-
leggedly walks into the saloon.

2   INT. SALOON - MED. CLOSE SHOT AT DOOR

Curly comes through the swinging doors swaggering as he walks.
CAMERA PANS WITH HIM as he passes a pretty dance hall girl
talking to a man. Curly calls out a jaunty greeting.

                CURLY
        Hiya, Babe?

He tips his hat taking it at the crown and as he raises the
hat the brim remains in place. He replaces the crown as he
walks on, CAMERA PANNING WITH HIM as he passes a couple of
tables where we see Western characters. In the background
against the wall Curly approaches a clothes rack.

3   MED. CLOSE SHOT - CURLY

He removes the entire hat, hangs it on a peg, then removes
the spurs and hangs them up, then he pulls out the front of
his shirt tail, dropping it and we realize that it is an
apron. Curly picks up a towel, throws it across his arm and
now we know that he is a waiter in the saloon.

A big burly man of the western gambler type, steps up behind
Curly and glares at him. Curly turns, reacts, smiles a
friendly smile and does his goofy wave.

                CURLY
        Howdy, boss,

3   CONTINUED:

                              BOSS (JACK)
                    Late again, eh?

                              CURLY
                    Well, I couldn't help it -- Silver
                    had a flat tire.

                              JACK
                    I'll give you a flat tire! Go on,
                    get busy!

He gives Curly a vicious kick in the seat. Curly hurries
out of scene. (NOTE: DURING THIS ENTIRE SEQUENCE WE HAVE
HEARD THE SINGING OF A MIXED CHORUS.)

4   MED. SHOT OF SALOON

We see a couple of tables in f.g. where western characters
are listening to the music which comes from Moe, Larry and
three girls, who stand in an old-fashioned pose while a
pianist at an old broken down piano clanks away at an ac-
companiment. They are singing, "She'll be comin' round the
mountain." Curly takes his place between Larry and Moe and
picks up the song.

5   MED. CLOSE SHOT - OF GROUP

As they sing.

6   CLOSE THREE SHOT - STOOGES

The group singing, "She'll be comin' round the mountain."
Curly throws in an interlude of his own arrangement.

                              CURLY (very quickly)
                    Oh yes, she'll be comin' round the
                    mountain, she will, she will, she
                    will. She'll be comin' round the
                    mountain when she comes, when she
                    comes, when she comes --

Moe gives him a smack without looking at him.

                              ENTIRE GROUP
                    She'll be comin' round the mountain
                    when she comes --

The Stooges and fellow actors singing, "She'll Be Coming Around the Mountain."

6   CONTINUED:

>   CURLY (singing interlude)
>   I just got through sayin' she'll be
>   comin' round the mountain, she'll
>   be comin' round the mountain, she'll
>   be comin' round the mountain -- oh
>   yeah, man!

Moe and Larry without looking, each bat him in the eye with
a fist.

>   MOE
>   What's the idea?

>   CURLY
>   I'm late so I'm making up what I
>   missed.

>   ENTIRE GROUP (singing)
>   She'll be comin' round the mountain,
>   she'll be comin' round the mountain,
>   she'll be comin' round the mountain
>   when she comes.

>   CURLY (ending up with)
>   If --

Larry and Moe look at him.

>   MOE
>   What do you mean "if"?

>   CURLY
>   If she don't fall off.

Moe gets him by the ears and twists. Suddenly Moe looks off,
reacts and draws the boys' attention to something o.s.

7   <u>CLOSEUP - CURLY</u>

     INTERCUT foregoing action.

8   <u>MED. SHOT - GROUP</u>

     The three girls are bowing to very slight applause as the
     boss approaches them and starts to bawl them out.

9   <u>CLOSE SHOT - JACK AND THE GIRLS</u>

>   JACK
>   That was awful! You sound like
>   three sick heifers!

Curly taking a bit of Stooges punishment: (a) First, a slap in the face,

(b) Curly retaliates with a burst of derby-hat machine gun fire,

(c) then an eyepoke which reveals Moe's tricky, darting fingers are in reality slapping Curly on the brow as they always did in every eyepoke.

9   CONTINUED:

                          1ST GIRL
          But we're doing our best.

                          JACK
          Well, you'll have to do better, or
          I'll put you to work in the kitchen.

Jack exits as the three Stooges step in. The girls are nearly
in tears.

                          MOE
          Don't let him talk to you like
          that, girls? Why don't you quit?

                          1ST GIRL
          We can't quit. Father's indebted
          to him and if we don't work it out
          he'll put father in jail!

The girls all stifle back a sob. The boys look at them then
each takes a girl's hand.

                          MOE
          There, there, now! Don't let it
          get you down.

                          LARRY
          Certainly. We love you.

                          CURLY
          Soon as we get enough money we'll
          pay off the old debt and take you
          out of this joint.

The girls smile happily.

10   MED. LONG SHOT

     The boys are still consoling the girls, patting their hands,
     etc., when Jack steps into scene menacingly and confronts
     the boys.

                          JACK
          Come on, get busy!

He hands Curly a metal tray then shoves Moe and Larry out
of scene, admonishing them to go to work as he follows them
out. Curly looks after Jack angrily, then turns back to the
girls.

                          CURLY
          He can't talk to us like that,
          the big bully!

10   CONTINUED:

    Jack steps back into scene, behind Curly. Curly, unaware
    of Jack's presence, continues his bragadocio manner.

               CURLY
        I don't care if he is the boss,
        he can't bluff me. One of these
        days I'll break --

    He tries to pantomime break but the tray hampers him. He
    turns and sees Jack but does not recognize him; hands Jack
    the tray.

               CURLY
        Here - - hold this.
          (he turns back to girls)
        I'll break him in two -- like this --

    He makes a motion of breaking something in two then suddenly
    he does a delayed take, and faces Jack; waves at him very
    friendly-like. Jack brings the tray down on Curly's head,
    bending it.

               JACK
        One more crack out of you and I'll
        break you in pieces. Go on, get
        busy!
          (shoves Curly out
          of scene, then turns
          on the girls)
        You too!

11   CLOSEUP - CURLY AND JACK

    INTERCUT foregoing action.

12   MED. SHOT AT BAR:

    Curly comes in, starts to wipe off the bar.

13   CLOSEUP - MOE

    He is standing at a table, taking an order. Moe turns toward
    the bar and yells:

               MOE
        One beer!

Our "heavy" Jack, having a tough time keeping a straight face at the sight of Curly with a tray wrapped around his shaven head. It was tough to keep from laughing during the making of a Stooges comedy, but even a smile would mean a retake and poor Curly would have to get clobbered again.

190

14   CLOSEUP - CURLY

    He repeats the order then turns and draws a stein of beer.
    He then turns and holding the glass in his hand, calls out:

                    CURLY
           One beer -- coming up!
             (calls signals)
           Forty-nine - sixteen - thirty-three -
           hike!

    He tosses the glass of beer like a foreword pass.

15   CLOSEUP - MOE AT TABLE

    The beer comes sailing into scene. Moe catches it without
    spilling a drop. He places it in front of the customer.

16   CLOSEUP - LARRY AT NEXT TABLE
    He is also taking an order, then turns toward the bar and
    calls out:

                    LARRY
           One beer!

17   CLOSEUP - CURLY AT BAR

    He repeats the order.

                    CURLY
           One beer coming up!

    He draws another beer, repeats the previous action, calling
    the signals and throws the glass of beer.

18   MED. CLOSE SHOT - LARRY AND MOE

    The beer comes flying into scene. Larry catches the mug by
    the handle, his arm swinging wide as if to stop the shock
    of the beer mug, and dumps the contents on Moe who is in
    line with the glass.

19   CLOSEUP - MOE

    He fries, then takes the beer mug by the handle as Larry
    enters and comes up to wipe Moe's face, apologizing.

In this scene, Curly tosses a beer glass which
sails through the air, landing with an almost too
perfect catch by Moe. I could swear this was
done with wires but for the life of me couldn't
find a wire as I scrutinized the frames. Moe
reacts in anger when Larry catches a glass full
of beer and douses him with the contents. His
facial expression, in the vernacular of show
biz, is described as "a slow burn."

One can almost feel what is coming by the expression on Moe's face as Larry says, "I'm sorry, Moe." If you look closely in the scene with Moe whacking Larry over the head with the beer mug, you will see that the glass is a "breakaway glass," scored and then painted so that it will crack easily but not shatter or harm the recipient when used for slapstick punishment. Larry went through a similar scene in a TV pilot made in the sixties titled *Three Stooges Scrapbook*. In this scene Norman scored and painted a vase with the wrong type of paint, which filled in the score marks. When Larry was whacked the vase refused to break. After receiving repeated blows to the head trying to get a good "take," Larry remained wobbly for hours.

19 CONTINUED:

                    MOE
          Aw, think nothing of it, kid. I know.
          It was an accident.

Suddenly Moe brings the beer mug down on Larry's head with
a crash.

                    MOE (scowling)
          That was no accident.

20 MED. SHOT OF SALOON (SHOOTING TOWARD SWINGING DOORS)

We see Jack in f.g. playing Solitaire. Behind him the doors
open and a western character, Pete, bespattered with dust,
enters and hurries to Jack. Jack turns and sees him.

                    JACK (sotto voce)
          Did you knock off that bank?

                    PETE
          Did I! I got forty grand.

                    JACK
          Good. Now listen....

He leans over and starts to whisper to Pete.

21 MED. CLOSE SHOT AT BAR

The three Stooges are busy behind the bar. Curly takes a
glass and a bottle of Seltzer and starts preparing a drink.
He squirts Seltzer in the glass then reaches for a huge pair
of ice tongs (like ice men use) and drops a couple of ice
cubes into the glass. He then fills the glass with more
Seltzer. As he raises it Moe asks:

                    MOE
          Hey, what kind of a drink is that?

                    CURLY
          It's my own brand -- a Western Surprise.

                    MOE
          But it hasn't got whisky in it.

                    CURLY
          That's the surprise! Knk! knk! knk!

As he chuckles Moe hits the bottom of the glass which
causes the contents to fly up into Curly's face.

22   <u>BIG CLOSEUP - PETE AND JACK AT TABLE</u>

Jack is finishing his instructions to Pete.

> JACK
> We'll take the dough up to Little Lake
> and bury it later. In the meantime
> act like nothing happened. Go to the
> bar and buy yourself a drink.

Pete nods and exits.

23   <u>MED. CLOSE SHOT - AT BAR</u>

Pete comes up to the bar and orders a drink. Moe pours him
a slug. Pete tosses off the drink and slaps a coin on the
counter. Moe picks up the coin and reacts.

> MOE
> Whew! A twenty-dollar gold piece!

Pete reacts as he realizes he has put down the wrong coin.
Larry and Curly cluster around to inspect the coin as Moe
continues:

> MOE
> Where'd you get this, pardner?

> PETE (furtively)
> Oh, I just dug it up.
> > (he grabs the coin, puts it back
> > in his pocket and hands over
> > a quarter)
> Thought it was a quarter.

He exits quickly. The boys look after him.

24   <u>CLOSE SHOT - THREE STOOGES</u>

> CURLY
> Dug it up? Gee! He must have
> found a gold mine!

> MOE
> If a dumbbell like that can strike
> gold so can we. Come on.

He starts to remove his apron.

> CURLY
> Oh, boy, we're gonna be gold diggers!

24   CONTINUED:

                              LARRY
          Gosh! We'll be rich overnight.

                              MOE
          Then we pay off the girls' debts and
          marry 'em.

                              CURLY
          Oh boy! I can just see it. Me
          coming home from a hard day's work -
          I whistle for my wife, and the dog
          comes out...
                    (he pauses to dream)
          ...Me with my own wife and my own
          children -- dozens of 'em.

                              MCE
          Dozens of them?

                              CURLY
          Yeah.

Moe gets his hand set, shows two fingers.

                              MOE
          How many is that?

                              CURLY
          That's two.

                              MOE
          Yeah!
                    (he jabs Curly in the eyes)
          Go on, get going! We got gold dig-
          ging to do.

Curly is waving at him furiously, as we -

                                        FADE OUT:

196

FADE IN: (DAY)

25   <u>EXT. LAKE SET - MED. CLOSE SHOT</u>

(LAKE SET ON STAGE #6, AS USED IN PROD. #444). We see
Jack, the saloon proprietor and Pete, his henchman. They
have dug a hole and are burying the money they robbed from
the bank. As Pete shovels the dirt in the ground, Jack
watches him.

                    JACK
           Reckon the stuff'll be safe
           here all right.

He takes a plug of tobacco and bites into it. Suddenly he
lets out a yell of pain and claps a hand to his mouth; then
sticks his finger in his mouth and speaks angrily.

                    JACK
           Doggone it! I lost a gold filling
           out of my tooth.

He starts to search for it as Pete stops him.

                    PETE
           We ain't got time to look for it
           now. Let's get back to town before
           we're missed. Come on.

Both men hurry from scene. CAMERA PANS WITH THEM as they
run off on the opposite side and disappear into the brush.

                          WIPE TO:

26   <u>MED. CLOSE TRUCKING SHOT</u> (DAY)

Three pairs of hip boots are wading across a shallow part
of the lake. CAMERA TRAVELS WITH THEM and TRUCKS BACK
disclosing a pack mule wearing hip boots on his front and
hind legs and Curly walking in the middle beside him, also
wearing hip boots. The mule is loaded down with a pack sky
high. A halter rope stretches out in front of him. CAMERA
PULLS BACK to a LONGER SHOT, revealing Moe and Larry.
They are dressed in screwy bathing suits, also hip boots,
and cowboy hats, and they are leading the mule. Beside
them trots a little dog and he is also loaded with a pack.
As the boys scramble up on to shore they stop and survey
the country. A ladder hangs on the side of the mule's pack.

                    MOE
    Whoa! Yorick.

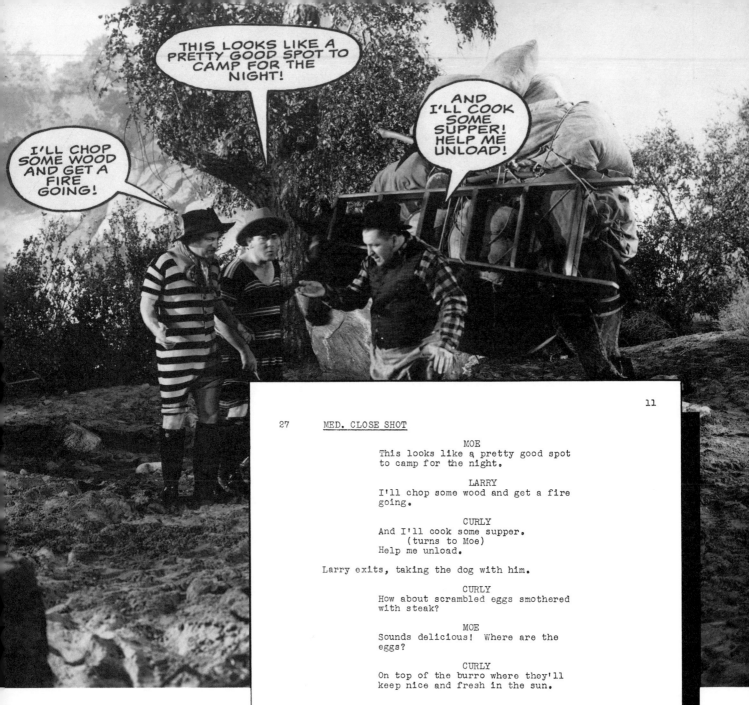

11

27   MED. CLOSE SHOT

                    MOE
              This looks like a pretty good spot
              to camp for the night.

                    LARRY
              I'll chop some wood and get a fire
              going.

                    CURLY
              And I'll cook some supper.
                    (turns to Moe)
              Help me unload.

      Larry exits, taking the dog with him.

                    CURLY
              How about scrambled eggs smothered
              with steak?

                    MOE
              Sounds delicious! Where are the
              eggs?

                    CURLY
              On top of the burro where they'll
              keep nice and fresh in the sun.

28   A WOODED SPOT - MED. SHOT (STG. 6)

      Larry is chopping wood. He smacks a branch which cuts
      off but flies up and comes down, conking Larry on the head.

29   MED. CLOSE SHOT

      Curly props the stepladder against the burro and climbs
      up to unload the provisions. He reaches for the eggs and
      carefully hands the package to Moe.

                    CURLY
              Fresh hen fruit! Handle with care!

      As Moe takes the package and starts away Curly pulls out
      a sack of flour and throws it down, yelling:

                    CURLY
              Sack of flour coming down!

      Moe turns quickly, sees the sack of flour coming and reaches
      out to grab it, dropping the eggs and catching the flour.
      He then looks down at the eggs and reacts.

30   <u>INSERT - PACKAGE OF EGGS</u>

Smashed open and little baby chicks coming out of the shells.
(NOTE: Be sure chicks are wet)

CONTINUATION SCENE 29:

Moe yells at Curly.

                  MOE
You broke the eggs, puddinhead!

                CURLY
So what? We'll have steak smothered
in lamb chops...

                  MOE
You fix it. I've got prospecting to
do. Hand me down the dynamite and
be <u>careful</u>!!

31   <u>CLOSE SHOT - CURLY ON LADDER</u>

                  CURLY
             (muttering)
I'll handle it as if it were eggs.
             (looks at smashed eggs -
              reacts)
I'll be careful.

He reaches up to the load for a box labeled "DYNAMITE" and
has difficulty extricating it. He tugs with all his might
then pulls the box of dynamite loose and almost falls backward as it slips out of his hands and goes sailing over
his head.

32   <u>SKY SHOT - OF DYNAMITE BOX</u>

Revolving around in the air, then descending.

33   <u>CLOSE SHOT - MOE</u>

He sees the dynamite in the air and runs over to catch it.
It drops into his arms and he grabs it just before it hits
the ground. He breathes a big sigh of relief then turns
angrily.

                  MOE
    Why you ---

He charges at Curly.

34   MED. CLOSE SHOT - CURLY ON LADDER (DOUBLE)

The burro becomes startled and starts moving out from under
the ladder. Curly frantically clutches the ladder. He yells
for help. As the burro moves away the stepladder topples
to the ground and Curly pulls the load of provisions down
on top of himself.

35   CLOSEUP - CURLY

Under the pile of provisions. He comes up with a stew pot
over his head, the handle sticking crazily out, and pulls it
off with a "PLOP" caused by the vacuum.

                                        WIPE TO:

36   EXT. CAMP SET - MED. SHOT

Moe is near a clump of rocks in the b.g. and Curly in the
f.g. has a side of beef on an upturned grocery box.

                         CURLY
              Knk! knk! knk! Thin steaks are
              the tenderest.

He wields a big cleaver and proceeds to cut off very thick
steaks from the side of beef.

37   WOODED SPOT - MED. SHOT (STG. 6)

Larry is chopping wood. As he brings the axe down, it splits
a small log and goes into a rock on which the wood was
resting.

38   CLOSEUP - LARRY

He brings up the axe and looks at it. It is bent cockeyed.

BACK TO SCENE 37:

Larry picks up the rock and tosses it over his shoulder.

39   EXT. CAMP SET - CLOSEUP CURLY

The rock hits Curly on the head. He reacts as he sees what
hit him, turns, sees:

40   CLOSE SHOT - MOE AT ROCKS

He throws a rock aside, then lights a stick of dynamite.

41   CLOSEUP - CURLY

Curly seeing Moe throw a rock thinks Moe threw the one that
hit him. Angrily he throws at Moe.

                         CURLY
                Here! See how you like it!

42   EXT. CAMP SET - CLOSE SHOT - MOE

The rock flies into scene and hits him on the head. Moe
grabs his head in pain, looks off as Curly's voice comes
over:

                         CURLY'S VOICE
                Take that!

                         MOE
                Oh yeah!

Without thinking he throws the lighted stick of dynamite
at Curly.

43   MED. SHOT
      (showing the mule behind Curly)

Curly ducks as the dynamite flies through the scene and
lands in front of the mule.

44   BIG CLOSEUP - CURLY

He looks toward the mule then screams.

                         CURLY
                Run for your life, Yorick!
                It's dynamite.

Curly exits.

45   CLOSEUP - THE MULE

He looks down at the sputtering dynamite, watches it
curiously.

RUN FOR
YOUR LIFE,
YORICK!
IT'S
DYNAMITE!

46   <u>MED. SHOT - CURLY</u>

As he rushes to Moe.

> CURLY
> Quick! We gotta get some water
> and put it out before it goes off.

He and Moe run around like chickens with their heads off,
then grab a bucket, each going in the opposite direction
with the same bucket, etc., until finally they both run
off together.

47   <u>CLOSEUP - THE DOG</u>

He is asleep. He wakes up, reacts as he sees:

48   <u>CLOSE SHOT - YORICK</u>

Munching the grass and paying no attention to the splutter-
ing dynamite beside him. Strongheart runs in, picks up the
stick of dynamite and trots over to the box of meat, CAMERA
PANNING WITH HIM, drops the dynamite into the box and trots
away.

49   <u>MED. CLOSE SHOT - MOE & CURLY</u>

They run in with a bucket of water splashing as they go.

50   <u>MED. SHOT OF MULE</u>

Moe and Curly run in and stop at the mule as Larry rushes
in. They react as Curly exclaims:

> CURLY
> Look! The dynamite's gone!
> Yorick must have eaten it.

51   <u>CLOSE SHOT - THE MULE</u>

Moe enters and places his ear to the mule's side, listening fearfully. Curly and Larry come into scene, also
listening to the mule. They hear a gurgling sound.

52   <u>INSERT: - THE MEAT BOX</u>

The dynamite fuse sputtering.

BACK TO SCENE 51:

                      CURLY
              Do you hear what I do?

                      MOE
              He swallowed it all right.
              I can hear it sizzling!

Curly reacts and WOO WOO'S.

                      MOE
              Quick! The water!

They hurry to the mule's head. Moe and Curly try to force
open the burro's mouth as Curly stands ready to pour the
water down.

                      CURLY
              Don't be a stubborn mule, you
              jackass! Take this or you'll
              explode!

                      MOE
              When I open it, you throw the
              water in his mouth.

53   CLOSEUP - CURLY

                      CURLY
              Okay! I'll take dead aim!

He aims.

54   MED. FULL SHOT

Moe and Larry open the mule's mouth; Curly throws the water,
dousing them.

55   CLOSEUP - MOE AND LARRY
      (dripping)

                      MOE
              I'll murder you!

56   MED. SHOT

Curly starts to run with Moe and Larry after him. The mule
runs from the scene.

57   MED. CLOSE SHOT - NEAR CLUMP OF ROCKS

      Curly runs in as Moe and Larry enter and grab him. They
      start to work out on Curly twisting his ears, etc.

58   CLOSE SHOT - OF MEAT BOX

      Showing the stick of dynamite with the fuse almost entirely
      burned away. It explodes.

59   MED. CLOSE SHOT - MOE, CURLY AND LARRY (ROCK CLUMP)

      The explosion is heard and a shower of dirt, rocks, canned
      food, then pieces of meat, the ragged SIDE OF BEEF, etc.,
      hit the Stooges. They stare down at the meat, pick up
      several big pieces, inspect them and then look at each other.
      Then they look at the spot where the mule was last seen.

60   MED. SHOT

      Showing the mule has disappeared. The meat box is in
      pieces and a hugo gaping hole is seen in the earth. Wisps
      of smoke drift from the wreckage.

CONTINUATION SCENE 59:

                          MOE
                Alas, poor Yorick, I knew him well.

                          LARRY
                Poor Yorick --

                          CURLY
                -- gone with the wind - pfft!

      They bring out big red bandanas from their pockets and blow
      into them loudly.

                     XXX FAST TEMPO XXX

61   CLOSE SHOT - STOOGES

                          MOE
                     (facing Curly)
                It's all your fault. If you hadn't
                hit me with that rock I wouldn't
                have thrown the dynamite and we'd
                still have poor Yorick.

61 CONTINUED:

    Moe jabs Curly in the eyes, then smacks him, knocking him
down. Curly puts his hands out to protect the fall, then
lets out a yell as his hands land on the ground. He brings
up his hand and looks at it.

62   <u>INSERT - CURLY'S HAND</u>

The gold filling stuck to it.

               CURLY'S VOICE
      Look! A gold nugget shaped like
      a tooth! We've struck solid gold!

63   <u>CLOSE THREE SHOT</u>

             LARRY
      Oh boy -- gold!

Moe grabs the filling and looks at it.

             MOE
      Solid gold -- fourteen karat!

             CURLY
      Carrots? That don't look like
      vegetables to me.

Moe lets him have the two fingers in the eyes.

             MOE
      Go on, get busy!
        (turns to Larry)
      Go get the tools.
        (Larry rushes out.)
      Come on, puddinhead -- dig!

Moe and Curly start digging with their hands, like dogs,
throwing the dirt up in the air behind them.

64   <u>CLOSEUP - DOG</u>

Its ears go up.

65   <u>CLOSE SHOT - MOE AND CURLY</u>

Digging furiously, like dogs.

66   CLOSE SHOT - DOG (REVERSE ACTION)

The dog keels over backward and passes out.

67   MED. SHOT - CURLY AND MOE

still digging as Larry rushes in, his arms loaded with three
picks and shovels. The boys stand up and look at Larry.

                    LARRY
          Here's the tools.

                    MOE
          Drop 'em.

Larry drops the tools on Moe's foot.

The Stooges are digging like dogs when the real dog keels over at the sight of them. I realized that Jules's love for animals was in evidence again. Only this time, to make it easier, Jules has used a still for the frame where the dog winds up on his back.

68   INSERT - MOE'S FOOT

The tools land on it.

69   BIG CLOSEUP - MOE

There are tears in his eyes as he reacts in pain.

70   MED. SHOT

Moe starts to dance on one foot, jumping up and down. Larry
and Curly begin to clap time. Then Larry and Curly start
dancing as Moe stops to watch them. He steps up to them
angrily.

                    MOE
          Hey, come here, you guys.

Curly and Larry step up to him innocently. Moe bangs their
heads together and as they straighten up he gives them the
double slap.

                    MOE
          Go on! Quit pickin' on me and dig
          in the ground. Get busy!
                (to Larry)
          Hey, porcupine -- go and get the
          screen!

Larry runs out of scene. Moe takes a pick, turns and starts
to dig the ground, bending down close to it. Curly, behind
him, picks up a pick, swings it behind him also close to
the ground. The pick hits Moe in the fanny. Moe turns on
Curly angrily. He brings his pick down on Curly's head with
all his might. Curly grabs his head and begins to squawk.

71   CLOSEUP - MOE

As he reacts at the pick head, then brings it into scene
and reveals it, all bent out of shape like a corkscrew.

72   MED. TWO SHOT

Angrily Moe takes Curly's pick away from him and with one
vicious swing, he buries the head in the ground.

73   MED. CLOSE SHOT - MOE AND CURLY
Moe tugs at the pick in the ground. Suddenly the pick comes
out of the ground, the sharp end of the pick head having
pierced a stack of paper money.

74   CLOSEUP - MOE

He takes it big and reacts at the paper money.

75   INSERT - OF MONEY

stuck to the pick head.

76   MED. SHOT

Moe and Curly react excitedly as Larry comes in with the
screen (a gravel screen).

                    MOE (excitedly)
          We've struck it rich! We've struck
          pay dirt!

                    CURLY
          Pay dirt nothin'! We've struck a
          mint!

Moe grabs a shovel and digs into the ground. As he tries
to lift the shovel it is stuck. Moe starts to yank on the
shovel with all his might.

77   CLOSE TWO SHOT

As Moe yanks the shovel gives way, the butt end of it hitting Curly on the nose. Curly turns on Moe sore as hell.

                    CURLY
          What're you trying to do -- break
          the shovel?

                    MOE
          Go on! Keep digging before I
          murder you.

He threatens Curly.

78   MED. SHOT

Curly digs his shovel in but comes up with what appears to
be dirt. Larry has the screen ready over two bags. Curly
turns, throwing the dirt into the screen. Larry starts to
strain it.

79   INSERT OF THE SCREEN

As the dirt is shaken off revealing gold coins.

80   CLOSEUP - LARRY

He lets out a yell.

                    LARRY
          Look! Gold coins! Oh boy!

He drops the screen, rushes over to the hole that the boys
have dug, reaches in and comes up with a couple of bags of
gold.

81   CLOSEUP - LARRY

As he pulls the gold out and reacts Moe and Curly dive in
beside him. They also reach in the hole at the same time,
their hands getting twisted, each trying to beat the other.
Finally Curly comes out with a big stack of bonds.

                    CURLY (excitedly)
          Look! A lot of pretty papers!

                    MOE
          Them ain't papers, you sap -- them
          are bonds.

                    LARRY
          Who ever heard of bonds comin' out
          of the ground.

                    MOE
          Why not? They're gold bonds.

                    CURLY (excitedly)
          Bonds! Oh boy, ain't nature wonderful!

                    MOE (excitedly)
          Come on, we gotta get back to town
          and stake our claim.

Quickly they start up.

82   MED. LONG SHOT

The boys jump up from the ground, each grabbing some of the
money, then rush to the screen, each grabbing handfuls of
the gold coins which they shove in their pockets until they
have retrieved all of the coins, and money. Now as they
start to move away from the CAMERA the weight of the gold
coins, paper money and bonds cause their trousers to drop,
as we

                                        FADE OUT:

FADE IN: (DAY)

83   INT. SALOON - MED. FULL SHOT (SHOOTING TOWARD DOORS)

The place is empty. The swinging doors fly open and the
three Stooges enter, dressed to kill, Curly carrying a small
valise. They shout greetings to the girls, who rush forward to meet them.

84   MED. CLOSE SHOT - NEAR TABLE

The girls greet the boys effusively as Curly empties the
valise on the table, pouring a shower of coins, bags of
money, paper money and bonds on the table.

                    CURLY
          Knk! knk! knk! Well, we did it!
          Look, we're rich!

                    MOE
          Hurry up and change your clothes while
          we pay off your father's debt.

                    CURLY
          And then we'll be married.

He starts to sing "Rockabye Baby", swings an imaginary
baby, becomes shy, sticking his finger in his mouth. The
delighted girls throw their arms around the boys and kiss
them.

                    GIRLS (ad lib)
          It's wonderful!
          Our heroes!
          We'll be right back!

They hurry out of scene as Jack enters followed by Pete.
They react in amazement as they see the pile of wealth on
the table.

85   CLOSE GROUP SHOT

                    MOE
          We told you we'd make good.

                    CURLY
          Forty thousand bucks!

He snaps his fingers in the proprietor's face. Jack stares
wide-eyed, then picks up several of the bonds and examines
them. He thrusts them in the Stooges' faces.

                    JACK
          So you dug up stocks and bonds too, eh?

The Stooges nod smilingly. Jack exchanges looks with Pete
and the two reach for their guns.

85 CONTINUED:

> JACK (menacingly)
> Stand back from that table, you crooks!
> That's our dough.

86   <u>MED. SHOT</u>

As the bandits pull out their guns Curly quickly gives each of them the fingers in the eye. They howl with pain, grab their eyes as Moe and Larry scoop up the money and dump it in the valise. Curly tips the table over on the bandits, knocking them off balance and the three boys scramble out of scene. The bandits tear after them.

87   <u>MED. SHOT - AT STAIRCASE</u>

The three Stooges dash up the staircase closely followed by the two bandits who are firing wildly. The three boys run into a room and slam the door behind them.

88   <u>INT. ROOM - MED. SHOT</u>

The Stooges enter, barricade the door with a chair and Curly sits in it while Moe and Larry tear across the room to a window where they look out.

89   <u>EXT. WINDOW - DOWN SHOT</u> (WESTERN STREET)

(Taking in what seems to be the back of a horse just below the window).

90   <u>INT. ROOM - MED. SHOT</u>

Moe and Larry climb out on the ledge and jump just as the two bandits charge into the room, upsetting Curly who lands behind the door. Curly sees the bandits, sneaks up and swipes them across the face with the valise, which comes off the handle. This is unnoticed by Curly who still clutches the handle as he jumps out the window, following Moe and Larry. The two bandits react as they see the valise. They pick it up.

> JACK
> Come on! The car's downstairs.

They bolt out through the door.

In this scene the script calls for the Stooges to jump off a roof and land on the back of a horse. In order to protect the lives of our heroes, we have a very interesting use of doubles. In the first frame we see Moe and Larry approaching the edge of the roof, in the second frame Moe's double jumps onto the horse with Larry's double following closely behind him, in the third frame Larry and Moe's double are in the saddle and Curly's double is about to jump off the roof. This is all done very rapidly (sometimes the action is speeded up) and the end result looks like the real thing.

213

91   EXT. SALOON - CLOSE SHOT STOOGES

Seated on back of horse. They are riding like mad. CAMERA
PULLS BACK revealing the boys astride a PROP horse, used as
an advertisement by a saddle maker. Moe, in the middle,
turns to Curly, who is on the rear of the horse.

                         MOE
            Is the dough safe?

                         CURLY
            Soitanly! Look!

He brings the handle of the valise up and both react as they
see the valise is missing. Moe starts to bat Curly, then.
checks himself as they both look off.

92   EXT. STREET - MED. FULL SHOT

Jack and Pete with the valise are climbing into a Ford
touring car with the top down. The car starts forward.

93   EXT. SALOON - FULL SHOT

The three Stooges see the car as it passes them and react.

                         MOE
            There they go!

Curly takes a rope from the side of the horse, twirls it
over his head and throws it out of scene toward the moving
automobile.

94   MED. SHOT - REAR OF CAR

The rope comes in and catches on the spare tire carrier.

95   FULL SHOT - THE PROP HORSE

The rope tightens pulling the horse with the three Stooges
out of the scene.

96   MED. TRAVELING SHOT (PROCESS)

The PROP horse being pulled, the Stooges astride, reacting as
they see their predicament.

97 CLOSEUP - TRAVELING SHOT OF THE BANDITS (PROCESS)

They look back and react.

                    JACK
          Look! They're following us on
          horseback!

He draws a gun and fires.

98 CLOSE SHOT - STOOGES ON PROP HORSE (PROCESS)

Bullets fly in as the Stooges try to dodge them. Curly's
hat flies off as a shot whizzes through.

99 CLOSE SHOT - BANDITS (PROCESS)

Jack driving, Pete firing at the Stooges.

100 CLOSE SHOT - CURLY (PROCESS)

He holds his head and yells in pain.

                    CURLY
          I'm shot!

He removes his hand revealing a streak creased down the
middle, the crease still smoking.

101 LONG SHOT (LOCATION)

The bandits' car turns a corner on two wheels, the PROP
horse whipping around the turn also. (Use second Camera
from another angle so shot can be used twice.)

102 MED. TRAVEL SHOT (PROCESS)

The Stooges nearly fall off and Curly slides off the rear
of the horse but grabs the tail to keep from hitting the
ground.

103 MED. FULL SHOT (PROCESS)

Curly holding on to the horse's tail with his body flying
in the air. He "Woo woos" to Moe and Larry for help. They
turn around and react then reach out and clutch Curly,
trying to pull him back on the horse.

104 CLOSE SHOT - BANDITS IN CAR (PROCESS)

Jack is driving like mad while Pete empties his gun at
the Stooges.

PROCESS SHOT
A process screen of a western street is in evidence in the background of the frame on the left. The detailed explanation of the process shot can be found in this chapter in the section titled "About the Film."

215

WOO WOO WOO WOO!

In this scene the prop department has come up with a very poor example of a Curly dummy which Moe and Larry use to simulate Curly's falling off the horse. The next cut has Curly holding onto the horse's tail. This scene was shot on a process stage with a clip of a western town used for the background on the process screen. The third cut is a close-up of Curly "woo-wooing" as the buildings whizz by, giving one the feeling that Curly is being dragged through town as he holds on for dear life to a horse's tail.

217

MED. CLOSE SHOT - STOOGES (PROCESS)

Moe and Larry finally pull Curly back on the horse. As
they straighten up an overhanging branch from a tree nearly
knocks them off the horse. The branch snaps off and falls
into Curly's hand.

CLOSE SHOT - CURLY (PROCESS)

He recovers himself, disengages a hornet's nest from the
branch and throws the branch away.

                    CURLY
          Look -- a hornet's nest!
               (he gets an idea)
          One beer coming up.

                    MOE
          Thirty-eight -- nineteen -- hike!

Curly tosses the hornet's nest to Moe. Moe tosses it
toward the car.

INT. CAR - MED. CLOSE SHOT BANDITS (PROCESS)

The nest lands in the front seat between the two bandits.
The hornets swarm out, buzz around and sting the crooks, who
yell as they fight them off. Jack loses control of car.

FULL SHOT

The car careens crazily, still pulling the PROP horse and
Stooges behind it. Suddenly the car leaps a curb and heads
toward the side of a building marked "ALKALI COUNTY JAIL".

INT. JAIL - MED. SHOT (CELL IN B.G.)

The sheriff is seated behind a desk in f.g. The car crashes
through the side wall and the two bandits are knocked cold
by the debris and plaster from the crash.

MED. CLOSE SHOT

As the sheriff approaches the car the three Stooges come
tearing in.

                    SHERIFF
          What's going on here?

                    MOE (indicating bandits)
          Those dirty crooks stole our dough.

He pulls the valise out of the car.

A bit more of Hollywood trickery in this scene where a car is supposed to crash through a jail wall. In the first frame the car pulls up close to the wall. CUT away to inside the jail. A trough of flash powder is ignited under the camera. When the smoke clears the car is inside with debris and Stooges scattered in every direction.

219

In the script we have the film ending after Moe hits Curly over the head with a brick. Curly, in the actual film, after being clobbered by the brick, raises his head up one last time, grins and ad libs the single word, "Bonanza," as we FADE OUT.

110 CONTINUED:

> SHERIFF
> Your dough?
> > (he looks in valise and
> > pulls out a bond)
> Why, this money was stolen from
> the First National Bank!

111   CLOSE SHOT - STOOGES

Moe takes it big.

> MOE
> How do you like that -- and I
> thought we had a bonanza!

> CURLY
> Yes, we have no bonanza!

Moe, who has a brick in his hand, crushes it into powder on
Curly's head, as we

> FADE OUT

> THE END

1962
The Year of
THE THREE STOOGES MEET HERCULES

Curly-Joe, Moe, Larry and Quinn Rediker being stalked by the evil Cyclops.

Moe, trying to calm a rambunctous crowd during a tour with Hercules.

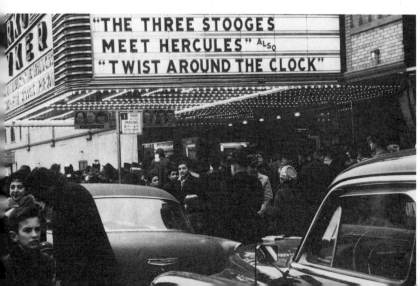

Three events that stood out during the making of *The Three Stooges Meet Hercules* were the trading of a Soviet spy for the release from a Russian prison of U-2 pilot Captain Gary Powers, the winning of the Nobel Peace Prize by Linus Pauling and the execution by hanging of Nazi war criminal Adolph Eichmann. These were major world events that the writers of Three Stooge comedies would probably have used as springboards for the two-reelers if Columbia had still been producing the shorts in 1962. But the time of the two-reeler had ended in 1958, and this was the year for Three Stooges features, something that Moe and Larry had constantly dreamed about during their twenty-five-year tenure at Columbia Pictures. Since 1958 they had already starred in *Have Rocket, Will Travel* for Columbia and *Snow White and the Three Stooges* for 20th Century-Fox. After the success of *Have Rocket* Columbia wanted to make a sequel but, despite the film's box office success, they refused to increase the Stooges' salaries and the boys turned down their offer. My husband, Norman, had created the story idea for *The Three Stooges Meet Hercules* and my father and his partners were determined to make it their next feature.

Unable to get the services of the Three Stooges, Columbia, without Moe, Larry and Curly-Joe's knowledge, began production on a feature film that consisted of a paste-job of old Stooge film clips titled *Stop! Look! and Laugh!*—an unauthorized Three Stooges film that was to lead, eventually, to Columbia's production of *Hercules*—on the Stooges' terms.

The year 1962 was also the thirty-fifth of the Academy Awards, with the winner of best picture David Lean's monumental classic, *Lawrence of Arabia*. And, of course, the monumental disaster of the year was *Cleopatra*, a super-colossal box office dud with a cost that came close to $40,000,000—an all-time record for the industry.

The Stooges in 1962 also had an industry record as the longest running comedy act in history, and among themselves they had their own personal record; they were now performing with their third "Curly" replacement, Jo-

Hercules doing sensational business due to the Stooges p.a. tour.

seph DeRita, nicknamed Curly-Joe, whose real name was Joseph Wardell.

Joe was born July 12, 1909, in Philadelphia, and was the only one of the Stooges who came from a show business background. His mother, Florenz DeRita, was a dancer, and his father, Frank Wardell, was a stage technician.

At age seven, Joe toured with his parents; then came seven seasons playing the title role in a stage version of *Peck's Bad Boy*. At eighteen, Joe decided to do a comedy single in which he sang and danced, and in 1921 he went into burlesque, since his type of vaudeville single-act had gone the way of the dinosaur. Joe continued to play the New Columbia Burlesque Circuit until 1942, after which he moved to California to headline in a show at the Music Box Theatre in Hollywood. MGM, attracted by his good notices, signed him to a contract, and he made his film debut in the 1944 film *Doughgirls* with Ann Sheridan. This was followed by a stint for the USO, and in 1943 he starred in a series of two-reel comedies for Columbia.

During World War II, Joe worked for the USO and toured the South Pacific with his good friend Randolph Scott as his straight man. On another tour, to entertain servicemen in England and France, Joe went overseas with Bing Crosby as his straight man. Upon his return to the States, he played the Hollywood Casino in Los Angeles and made guest appearances on many popular radio shows of the day. Before joining the Stooges in 1958, he had a major role as the "hangman" in *The Bravados* for 20th Century-Fox and then became a steady in Minsky's burlesque show in Las Vegas. But it was as Curly-Joe and in association with the Three Stooges that DeRita attained the stardom and acclaim he had always longed for.

Retired today, Joe leads a rather quiet life, spending most of his time watching television and listening to classical music. He resides presently in North Hollywood with his wife Jean, whom he married in 1966.

When I called Joe to ask him questions about the sixties, he came up with a humorous anecdote which took place when the Stooges were playing the Police Circus in St. Louis.

The Stooges Meet Hercules *and the fans meet the Stooges on an RKO tour in 1961.*

Did you say fly the friendly *skies?*

225

The McKeever twins have changed from their Cyclops makeup and are now Roman guards, much to the Stooges' displeasure.

The Stooges do a bit of promo for American Air Lines.

The boys were in their dressing rooms, which were in an unusual location in an area underneath the stadium. On this particular day, the Stooges were waiting for their turn on the bill. The area leading into the dressing rooms was jammed with spectators, fans and people hawking their wares. There was a knock at the door and Joe looked up to see a harried, breathless man walk through the door dragging a small boy behind him. He asked if the Stooges would mind having a picture taken with him and his son. Amidst the rush-rush and tumult of people entering and leaving, the Stooges patiently waited for the picture to be taken. After which the man left, dragging the youngster behind him. Fifteen minutes later, there was another knock at the door and the man entered again. Apologizing, and with a sheepish grin on his face, he explained that in the midst of the jumble of fans outside the door, he had grabbed the hand of the wrong little boy. He pointed at the smiling lad standing next to him, explained to the Stooges that *this* was his son and asked them to pose for the picture over again.

At the time that DeRita went on tour with Larry and Moe to promote *Hercules*, he was a neophyte with only four years in service with the Stooges. Curly-Joe was the baby of the group at fifty-three, with Larry an even sixty and Moe the senior citizen at sixty-five. These gentlemen were no chickens, and I refer both to their longevity and stamina. When you are past your prime, it is no easy task to bang, bop and run the slapstick gauntlet.

During the *Hercules* tour, sixty-five-year-old Moe was interviewed by James Ritch, who asked, "What's it like doing thirty years of pratfalls and how does it feel every day to take a hit on the head, a punch in the nose, a gouge in the eye, a kick in the pants, and an elbow to the ribs?"

"You get a little cagey," Moe answered. "We're not as violent as we used to be."

Through the sixties, I recall my father being very concerned about the violence in the old films, and when he started making features, he decided to clean up the act, violence-wise. He did feel though that the Stooges' form of savagery came across like an animated cartoon. It just wasn't real. In a Stooges comedy, when someone was whacked on the head and got back up instantly, neither moaning nor groaning and with no bloodshed, one had the feeling they were watching a cartoon with three, live Wiley Coyotes. And what their vast army of fans liked best about their three TV favorites was that they got the chance to meet these cartoons and shake their hands—which is something they did by the thousands during the super-successful *Hercules* tour.

My mother, Helen Howard, had her say about violence in the Stooges comedies when she wrote, "Although the PTA thought the comedies were too violent, the fan letters written by mothers across the country do not reflect this. They all remark how happy their children are watching the Stooges." She goes on to tell about a newspaper column she had read where a housewife who was interviewed on the street was asked, "How do you punish your children?" Her answer: "The worst thing I can do and the only thing that works is not letting my kids see the Three Stooges—they love them so."

Moe, when interviewed regarding the violence, said, "And now my own grandchildren watch us on television instead of Popeye and, so far, have had no ill effects." He went on to say, "I was so concerned about violence that I asked one little girl if she wasn't frightened when we started hitting each other. She said, 'Oh, no, you're just silly.' "

Larry, when interviewed one time regarding violence and injuries to the Stooges, reported that he had stepped into a punch in a gangster comedy, "It knocked my tooth right down my throat. I just gulped and swallowed it—I didn't want to ruin the take."

Although at its peak in the early sixties, the violence issue regarding the Stooges simmered down during the seventies and eighties and a generation of "baby boom" Stooges fans grew up to become very normal young people—perfectly wonderful doctors, lawyers, blue collar workers, white collar workers—even women by the thousands turned out to be Stooges fans.

By 1962, Moe had been married for close to forty years, with grown children and grandchildren, and one would think it would be time to retire, but he was the "original workaholic" and refused to give up acting—or the act.

And so, in this year of mythical adventure films, started by Joseph E. Levine with his blockbuster film *Hercules*, the Stooges, too, got a chance to participate in the classics, which they did in spades, in the fun romp *The Three Stooges Meet Hercules*.

It is interesting to note how the making of *Hercules* came about. Norman Maurer, recalling the success of Abbott and Costello's "meet" pictures, had offered Columbia *The Three Stooges Meet Hercules*. Despite the box office success of the Stooges' previous Columbia feature, *Have Rocket, Will Travel*, Columbia and the picture's producer, Harry Romm (who was also the Three Stooges' agent and personal manager), refused to improve the terms of their contract and, on Norman's advice, the boys stood firm, refusing to work for their old salary.

Columbia, unable to get the services of the Stooges and wanting desperately to cash in on the success of *Have Rocket* with a quick, inexpensive sequel, hired Harry Romm as the producer and proceeded to paste together a new Stooges feature with clips from their old shorts. It was titled, *Stop! Look! and Laugh!* and starred Paul Winchell.

The Stooges were furious. They fired Romm as their manager, sued Columbia and offered *Hercules* to American International Pictures, who leapt at the opportunity to make a low-budget feature with the hottest kids' property in the country.

But AIP had one condition, they wanted an Easter release of *Hercules*. Now integrity on the part of the Stooges stepped in. Norman had replaced Romm as their manager, and, since the Stooges were in the midst of shooting the Fox film, *Snow White and the Three Stooges*, for a summer release, they all felt it was unethical to have another studio jump the gun on Fox with an earlier release.

Norman and the Stooges turned down the AIP offer and proceeded with their litigation against Columbia. In a hearing at Los Angeles Superior Court, the evidence presented by the Stooges and Norman was so overwhelming

rjp   THE THREE STOOGES MEET HERCULES
                Revised Page --   115
                June 5, 1961

```
INT. ARENA - DAY

367    FULL SHOT (STOCK)                                      367
       The stands thronged with eager spectators.

368    ODIUS' BOX                                             368
       Odius occupies a front box under an ornamental canopy.
       Beside him sits Diane, expressionless as usual, in custody of
       the Matron.  Turning, Odius gives the signal to start the
       games.

369    HERALDS (STOCK)                                        369
       They raise their trumpets and blow a fanfare.

370    PANNING SHOT  HERCULES                                 370
       Hercules races his chariot onto the field, reining up his
       magnificent horses in a spectacular show of power.  Thunder-
       ing applause greets his showy entrance.  The hubs of the
       chariot are fitted with huge twisted steel blades, like can-
       openers.

370A   LOW ANGLE  EMPHASIZING THE MENACE OF THE CUTTERS       370A

371    STOCK SHOT  ARENA                                      371
       Again the Heralds raise their trumpets and blow a fanfare.

372    MEDIUM SHOT  ARENA GATEWAY                             372
       The gateway leads from the dungeon into the arena.  Schuyler
       and the Stooges trudge out, in chains, guarded by soldiers.
       In addition to wrist chains, the Stooges are hooked together
       by collar chains, and a guard pulls them along like dogs on
       a leash.  When they are well into the arena, the soldiers step
       back a few paces, leaving Schuyler and the Stooges on display
       for the spectators.

373    MEDIUM SHOT  SPECTATORS IN STANDS                      373
       Yelling for the fight to start -- some of them already turning
       thumbs down in anticipation of the slaughter.

374    MEDIUM CLOSE SHOT  ODIUS AND DIANE                     374
       Odius is smugly satisfied; Diane is expressionless and
       disinterested.

375    MEDIUM CLOSE SHOT  STOOGES AND SCHUYLER                375
       In the middle of the arena, reacting to the bloodthirsty
       reaction of the crowd.  Schuyler looks off, sees the royal
       box and recognizes Diane.
```

George Neise and Vicki Trickett in Odius' Box.

During the production of The Three Stooges Meet Hercules, *Norman Maurer, although busy as the film's producer, utilized his cartoonist's talents by drawing set sketches for many of the important scenes. It is intriguing to first view the script page and read the description after scene #368-ODIUS' BOX, then look at Norman's set sketch. From the script's brief description, Norman came up with the detailed drawing on the opposite page. The photographs on these two pages are scenes from the actual film and the shooting schedule covers the day that the scenes were shot. On the shooting schedule, under the heading EXT. ARENA, is scene #368 which was filmed on June 12, 1961. (The* Three Stooges Meet Hercules *was released in 1962.) It is also interesting to note the error on the first line of script page 115, "INT. ARENA-DAY." This should read, "EXT. ARENA-DAY." As you can see by the photographs, the scene in the arena was definitely shot out-of-doors, thus, the correct heading should read exterior or "EXT."*

228

Norman's set sketch of Odius' Box and the arena. This was a redress of the town square used in the Columbia feature Carmen *with Rita Hayworth.*

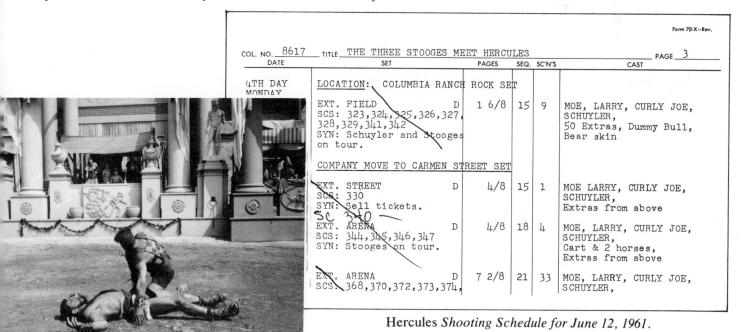

Quinn Redeker and Samson Burke in their big battle scene where Quinn (the pseudo Hercules) reforms Samson (the once-evil Hercules).

Form 70-X—Rev.

COL. NO. 8617   TITLE THE THREE STOOGES MEET HERCULES   PAGE 3

DATE	SET	PAGES	SEQ.	SC'N'S	CAST
4TH DAY MONDAY	LOCATION: COLUMBIA RANCH ROCK SET				
	EXT. FIELD D SCS: 323,324,325,326,327, 328,329,341,342 SYN: Schuyler and Stooges on tour.	1 6/8	15	9	MOE, LARRY, CURLY JOE, SCHUYLER, 50 Extras, Dummy Bull, Bear skin
	COMPANY MOVE TO CARMEN STREET SET				
	EXT. STREET D SCS: 330 SYN: Sell tickets.	4/8	15	1	MOE LARRY, CURLY JOE, SCHUYLER, Extras from above
	SC 340				
	EXT. ARENA D SCS: 344,345,346,347 SYN: Stooges on tour.	4/8	18	4	MOE, LARRY, CURLY JOE, SCHUYLER, Cart & 2 horses, Extras from above
	EXT. ARENA D SCS: 368,370,372,373,374,	7 2/8	21	33	MOE, LARRY, CURLY JOE, SCHUYLER,

Hercules *Shooting Schedule for June 12, 1961.*

260   CONTINUED: 260

                    THESUS (cont'd)
        physician? Never around when I --
                (to girls)
        Well? Well? Do something! Get
        me something for my seasickness!

One of the lovelies offers Thesus a large bunch of grapes. He
reaches for them eagerly.

                    THESUS
        Grapes! That's wonderful!
        That'll cure any --
                (suddenly checking
                 himsefl)
        Oh, no, no! Grapes! Who
        brought that up?

With a strangled cry, Thesus jumps up and runs to the nearest
railing.

                                        DISSOLVE TO:

EXT. DECK - DAY

261   MEDIUM SHOT (PROCESS)   261
        Schuyler and the Stooges face King Thesus, who is back on
        his improvised throne. The Captain looks on from b.g. as
        Simon waves toward Schuyler standing beside Curly Joe.
        The boys are unmanacled, but still have their leg irons.

                    SIMON
        That's the strong one, Sire!

                    CURLY JOE
                (indicating Schuyler)
        He means him.

                    MOE
                (barking)
        The King knows that, you knothead!

Moe threatens Joe, who shrinks away. Schuyler steps in front
of Thesus, who looks him over admiringly.

                    THESUS
        Oh my, he does look strong...
        Yes, indeed...I mean -- you're
        the one who rowed --
                (making rowing motion)
        Strong as twenty men! My...

When it came time for me to choose the illustrative material for the section on The Three Stooges Meet Hercules, *I remembered the sketches that Norman had hanging on the wall of his office. They are in full color and although rather rough and free in style, they definitely have a certain charm. Both the sketch of Odius' Box and the Deck of King Thesus' Galley were instrumental in improving the quality of production on this film. Norman made dozens of set sketches and a series of storyboards which went a long way toward giving this low-budget picture the look of a more expensive production.*

The Stooges and Hercules face King Thesus on his galley's deck.

Norman Maurer's set sketch of King Thesus' galley.

This Shooting Schedule dated 6/19/1961, which was also Moe's birthday.

The Stooges expound on the new-found strength of their man-made Hercules.

231

that the judge issued a temporary restraining order against Columbia which prohibited *Stop! Look! and Laugh!* from being shown in any theatre in the United States.

This temporary restraining order was issued forty-eight hours before the scheduled release of *Stop! Look! and Laugh!* Since Columbia had already spent a fortune in radio, TV, newspaper and other advertising, they were concerned over the tremendous monetary loss as well as a loss of face.

Now under the gun, Columbia brought in a dozen lawyers who worked through the night. By morning, they came up with a settlement offer for the Stooges. Columbia would reimburse them for all their legal costs and would agree to refrain from ever putting together another "paste-job" Stooges feature without the Stooges' participation, and they would make *The Three Stooges Meet Hercules*, accepting all of Norman's terms and with Norman as producer.

The picture came in at a budget of $420,000 and opened in Boston on February 15, 1962, at the Pilgrim Theatre. Throughout its release there were enormous crowds, with *Hercules* outgrossing the super-successful *Have Rocket, Will Travel.* It also outgrossed *Snow White and the Three Stooges*, theatre by theatre, despite the fact that *Snow White* was in color, was directed by Academy Award winner Walter Lang, and cost over $3.5 million dollars.

This latest, phenomenal Stooges resurgence of the early sixties was a shot in the arm for Moe and he often recalled with pleasure the many parents who would come up to him with their children in tow and say, "I knew the Stooges when I was a boy." In every instance their kids would look at their parents in total disbelief. One child told Larry, "Hey, I remember yesterday when Moe knocked you through the wall!" Ironically, yesterday was thirty years earlier.

The tour for *Hercules* took the Stooges to over twenty theatres in three days. Norman vividly recalled his touring days with *Hercules* in 1962 and was interviewed regarding his recollections in both *Moe Howard and the Three Stooges* and *Three Stooges Scrapbook*. In search of fresh material regarding what life was like during these Stooges promotion tours, I searched through my attic files and came across several crudely typed pages sent on to my father by either a fan or a reporter who followed the Stooges on their *Hercules* tour in the New York area. He wrote:

"Three fragile, old men, the last survivors from an era of vaudeville and burlesque, went from theatre to theatre to plug *The Three Stooges Meet Hercules*. This was a bus tour and the junket was comprised of the Stooges, their producer, twelve armed detectives and a bevy of smiling RKO theatre managers whose minds, concerned with the box office take, were praying for rain (so the fans would not go off to sun themselves at the local beaches).

"The reception the Stooges received was always the same: at least three thousand screaming kids outside the theatres (rain or shine), a blaring brass band with two or three satin-clad majorettes doing a rhythmic, pelvic twist, and then backstage, in a dimly lit area some little, old cleaning lady served cookies and Coke amidst the theatres' dangling ropes, curtains and props. The Stooges would wait backstage: Curly-Joe adjusting his cigar, Moe combing his hair over his forehead, Larry fluffing up his tousled mop and nursing a finger that had been scratched or bitten in the chaos outside. The children lucky enough to get in were out front watching the feature. They sat enraptured. When the screen finally dimmed at the end and the lights went up, a shrill cheer filled the auditorium as the Stooges entered. Their routine was short and on the surface nonsensical. But the nonsense had a surety about it and reminded one of Edward Albee speaking on the Theatre of the Absurd: 'Man's attempt to make sense for himself out of his senseless position in a world which makes no sense.' Almost eerily one felt the interplay was reminiscent of parts of *Waiting for Godot* and *Rhinoceros*. This was twelve minutes of theatre at its most absurd. Why not? This was the Three Stooges."

I wish I could write and congratulate the person who wrote the above story but, unfortunately, the letter was tucked away among my father's papers and there was no name or address attached to it.

Larry has that look in his eye but Moe and Curly-Joe know better than to mess with Samson Burke during a photo session.

To give a woman's perspective of life on tour, I searched my attic for my mother's diary and pored over her words regarding 1962 which chronicled all the ups and downs of this, the most exciting era in the Stooges' entire career. In her clear, crisp longhand she wrote of the days when the Stooges, after an extensive association with their manager-agent, Harry Romm, fired him because of the *Stop! Look! and Laugh!* episode:

"Moe's wife—that's me. That's the way I'm introduced. That's the name that gets the rise out of those I meet. And am I proud! But suddenly the Stooges become a piece of 'property' in the vernacular of show business. The hottest 'property' of the season. When this happens, a friend cannot be your agent and your agent is no longer your friend. Now the property becomes chopped liver and everyone is looking for his share. But with Moe sick in bed and all this going on, I wonder if it's all worth it."

In another entry she wrote:

"The most wonderful part of the entire tour is the love these children have for the Stooges—the fans. Their loyalty and love is an overpowering, suffocating force. What suddenly inspired this devotion? What a contribution to mankind that children are made to roll on the living room floor with joy while their mothers leave their dinner chores, drawn to the children, joining them in their hilarity and escaping from the daily monotonies of housework. The peals of laughter of little children—what a blessing."

As the *Hercules* tour continued she added:

"After the first show, which was a sell-out, Mabel, Larry, Moe and I were invited by a friend of our orchestra leader to an Italian restaurant for dinner. What a night! The restaurant was packed with gaping, awestruck children and adults. They crushed against us as we ate. Rumor has it that this restaurant is frequented by members of the Mafia. One man, who sat next to me during the meal, had gotten a bit tight. He expressed his love for the Stooges saying, 'If anybody hurta you, I'll bury 'em so deep they won't finda the hole.' "

The Stooges getting a triple headlock while Vickie Tricket and Quinn Rediker watch.

233

A Three Stooges Special Effect

The dictionary definition for the word special effect as it relates to motion pictures, is any artificial device that aids in producing a variety of illusions on the screen. In *The Three Stooges Meet Hercules* there are a number of these illusions and I have chosen just one of them for this section.

In my selected scene, our monster (a two-headed cyclops) who is actually a mere 6'3" is supposed to appear to be a twenty-foot giant with Moe looking doll-sized by comparison.

To achieve this effect, special effects-man, Dick Albain (the blonde gentleman in photograph #4, attempting to wire the back of Moe's costume) pulled a complicated routine out of his bag of tricks. The photographs on these pages show what difficulty one has to go to to achieve what appears to be a very simple illusion.

In photograph #8 the doll-sized Moe is really a doll. The model department borrowed the puppet head from Moe's 1947 merchandising item and had a miniature of Moe's costume constructed by the wardrobe department. The end result was a doll that really resembled Moe in long shots.

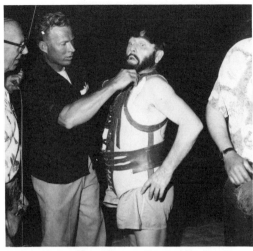

Moe with effects man, Dick Albain, being tucked into a leather harness to which wires will be attached.

Moe being helped into his costume.

Moe having trouble getting his arms through his shirt sleeves due to the restricting harness.

234

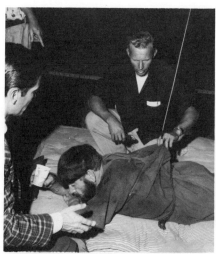

Producer, Norman Maurer watches Dick Albain wire Moe's duff for a bit of scary high wire work.

"Going Up!" And a nervous Moe does anything for a laugh.

Moe gets some last minute adjustments to his wiring by Dick Albain. The Siamese Cyclops appears on the process screen in the background.

Cyclops on the process screen in the background about to reach for the pint-sized "real" Moe, suspended high above the sound stage floor.

Cyclops holding the Moe doll for a long shot.

Close up of the Cyclops. Today's effects department would have had the eye rotating around in the forehead.

Our neophyte Cyclops getting some last-minute instructions for their scene from director Ed Bernds.

Hercules tour, the Stooges did a personal appearance at a club in Pittsburgh, and she wrote:

"Three weeks in Pittsburgh dragged on. It was quite boring to me and so confining and again I put aside my diary for there was nothing to record except to repeat myself. Work, eat, sleep for the 'boys,' and it was hard. Not only did the Stooges do their shows but they autographed thousands of photos and slips of paper and also sat for photographs with children. On looking back, I wonder why they did this. For what? They gave their all and the club owner was there to milk them dry. I guess that's life. The last three days they did one-nighters around Pittsburgh, but the steel strike started and so business was off. The last day they did some exploitation for their Hercules feature. We found out later it did terrific business."

That's Emil Sitka under the beard, trying to help the Stooges find their way. This must be a rehearsal, as both Moe and Larry are wearing bathrobes.

Producer Norman Maurer, trying to get someone's attention during production.

What fun it must have been to be married to a Stooge during those heady days of success, light years beyond anything the Stooges had previously experienced during their quarter century with Columbia. My mother lived in my father's shadow and loved every minute of it—well, almost. After completing the New York

The Stooges look mighty unhappy during this take. Is this the part they are playing or are their shoes too tight?

The Stooges getting ready to take a ride on a Time Machine.

The McKeever twins having facial hair applied while Larry does a bit of kibbitzing.

Emil Sitka and goat give this shot the appearance of a pastoral painting.

237

Moe tries his hand at a bit of direction.

On April 26th, in Detroit, Michigan, after several months of touring, my mother waited for my father to finish his work. Sitting in her hotel room, pen in hand, she put her thoughts to paper. Her writing took a sad and poignant turn which she expressed in poetry:

> Where are the buds that burst with pride
> Full of the joy of life inside?
> Where are the birds that chirp and sing?
> What's happened to me, I've lost a spring!
> Life's full of challenges that spur us fore,
> But as each is met we still find more.
> The victory of conquest, is this the thing,
> When out of my life I've lost a spring?
> The cheer of crowds and wild acclaim.
> The trip to the bank—monetary gain.
> My heart is sad, for what did it bring
> If I suddenly find, I've lost a spring?"

The year of *Hercules* was also the year of endless personal appearances at theatres, night clubs, circuses and state fairs, with TV appearances on shows starring Eddie Cantor, Danny

238   *Our Three Stooges are slaving away over a hot galley.*

The CAST SHEET comes in handy in case of emergency. I wouldn't try dialing any of those twenty-five-year-old phone numbers.

The Paramount Theater also bulged with Stooge fans in 1962.

CAST SHEET   JUNE 2, 1961

NORMANDY PRODS.   PROD. #8617

"THE THREE STOOGES MEET HERCULES"

CHARACTER	NAME	PHONE NO.
MOE	MOE HOWARD	GR 8-2245 & BR 2-9727
LARRY	LARRY FINE	HO 5-3171
CURLY JOE	JOE DERITA	PO 2-8969 & HO 9-2164
SCHUYLER	QUINN REDEKER	GR 96242 & CR 4-0201 &
DIANE	VICKI TRICKETT	HO 6-1508
DIMSAL-ODIUS	GEORGE NEISE	OL 7-1546 & OL 6-5300
HERCULES	SAMSON BURKE	EX 4-9235
ULYSSES	JOHN CLIFF	TH 6-5140
FIRST GUARD		
SECOND GUARD		
SIMON	GREG MARTELL	HO 9-2645
THESUS	HAL SMITH	GL 4-8125 & HO 4-5171
SHEPHARD	EMIL SITKA	MA 6-5625 & HO 5-3352
CAPTAIN	GENE ROTH	HO 5-9575
AJAX-CYCLOPS	MIKE McKEEVER	RI 7-3261
ARGO-CYCLOPS ACHILLES	MARLIN McKEEVER LEWIS CHARLES	GR 9-2516 OL 4-6529 & HO 3-4811 &
FREDDIE ANITA	ED FOSTER	DI 5-0568
HELEN HECUBA MATRON	DIANA PIPER	OL 66445
PHILO	RUSTY WESCOATT	HO 5-4091

Larry, Curly-Joe and Moe with hair neatly combed, pants neatly pressed, playing the perfect gentlemen.

CREW SHEET   JUNE 2, 1961

NORMANDY PRODS.   PROD. #8617

"THE THREE STOOGES MEET HERCULES"

PRODUCER	NORMAN MAURER	HF 0-5012
DIRECTOR	ED. BERNDS	ST 0-7495 & TR 3-2578
ASS'T DIRECTOR	HERB WALLERSTEIN	PO 1-1186
ASS'T DIRECTOR	PAT CORLETO	ST 4-5920
ART DIRECTOR	DON AMENT	WE 6-2063
SCRIPT SUPER.	CONNIE EARLE	PO 3-6376
CAMERAMAN	SCOTTY WELBORN	PO 9-2509
OPERATOR	VAL O'MALLEY	DI 5-6821
ASS'T CAMERAMAN	J. SAPIER	DI 7-1709
STILLMAN		
SOUND MIXER	J. FLASTER	CR 5-3834
RECORDER	ELDON COUTTS	CT 3-0369
MIKEMAN	F. MOOREHEAD	EM 4-1904
CABLEMAN	A. PAYNE	CT 4-5936
HEAD GRIP	AL BECKER	CR 5-6384
GAFFER	HOWARD ROBERTSON	HO 3-8661
BEST BOY	HENRY STEVENS	CL 5-2904
SET DRESSER	BILL CALVERT	CT 3-9730
PROP MAN	HARRY HOPKINS	PO 5-0360
2ND PROP MAN	CHARLES McCOY	
LEADMAN	IRVING GOLLFARB	
LADIES COSTUMER	PAT PAGE	
MEN'S COSTUMER	MOE FRIEDMAN	
HAIRDRESSER	JEAN AUSTIN	
MAKEUP ARTIST	JOE DI BELLA	
PROPSHOP MAN	DICK ALBAIN	
EDITOR	EDDIE BRYANT	

The CREW SHEET

"Day out of Days" lets you know just what dates you have to work.

NORMANDY PRODS.

47
12
95

M-61

DAY OUT OF DAYS

PRODUCER: NORMAN MAURER · ·   PROD. #8617 THE THREE STOOGES
                                             MEET HERCULES
DIRECTOR: EDWARD BERNDS · ·   SCHED. DAYS: 13 PLUS 1 PRE-PROD.
ASST. DIR: HERB WALLERSTEIN · ·   DATE TYPED: 5/31/61

CHARACTER	PRE-PROD	DAYS WORK	DAYS IDLE	TOTAL DAYS	START DATE	FINISH DATE
1. MOE · ·	1	13	0	14	6/6	6/23
2. LARRY · ·	1	13	0	14	6/6	6/23
3. CURLY JOE · ·	1	13	0	14	6/6	6/23
4. SCHUYLER · ·	1	13	0	14	6/6	6/23
5. DIANE · ·	1	10	3	14	6/6	6/23
6. DIMSAL-ODIUS · ·	1	10	3	14	6/6	6/23
7. HERCULES		6	2	8	6/8	6/19
8. ULYSSES		3	4	7	6/8	6/16
9. FIRST GUARD		3	2	5	6/12	6/16
10. 2ND GUARD		3	2	5	6/12	6/16
11. THESUS		2	0	2	6/16	6/19
12. SIMON		2	0	2	6/13	6/14
13. SHEPHERD		1	0	1	6/7	6/7
14. CAPT.		1	0	1	6/13	6/13
15. AJAX-CYCLOPS		1	0	1	6/7	6/7
PROCESS		1	0	1	6/20	6/20
16. ARGO-CYCLOPS		1	0	1	6/7	6/7
PROCESS		1	0	1	6/20	6/20
17. ACHILLES		1	0	1	6/23	6/23
18. FREDDIE		1	0	1	6/23	6/23
19. ANITA		1	0	1	6/16	6/16
20. HELEN		1	0	1	6/16	6/16
21. HECUBA		1	0	1	6/16	6/16
22. MATRON		1	0	1	6/16	6/16
23. PHIO		2	0	2	6/13	6/14

The author and sons Michael and Jeffrey on vacation at San Simeon (Hearst's Castle).

An interesting inter-office memo regarding stock footage used in The Three Stooges Meet Hercules.

An RKO tour is definitely not all work, as Moe, Larry and Curly-Joe relax with their fans.

FORM 11-4 50 RMS. 11-60

INTER-OFFICE COLUMBIA COMMUNICATION

To MARION MARKUS   From NORMAN MAURER
Attention of_____   By_____
In Regard to THE THREE STOOGES MEET HERCULES   Date December 20, 1960

Per our conversation regarding front office clearance on stock footage:

The following is tentatively planned for use in "The Three Stooges Meet
Hercules" - Production No. 8617-18.

1. YOU CAN'T TAKE IT WITH YOU:

Fireworks sequence and crowd re-actions.
Reel Five A
Scenes: 649, 658, 659, 660, 661, 662, 663, 664

2. SLAVES OF BABYLON:

Battle between armies - eclipse scene:
Reel Three A
Scenes: 28, 29, 30, 31, 32, 33, 34, 35, 36, 37, 38, 39, 40, 41

Den of Lions:
Reel Two B
Scenes: 47, 53

3. SALOME:

Heralds trumpeting atop a stone parapet:
Reel Two B
Scene: 30

Galley scenes - galley slaves rowing
Reel One B

Waterfront of small seaport:
Reel One B
Scene: 28

Townspeople storming palace gates:
Reel Five B
Scenes: Scattered cuts through Five B

NORMAN MAURER

NM/lfm

Thomas, Ed Sullivan, Ed Wynn and Steve Allen, to name just a few. During this period, the Stooges' careers expanded into other realms of creativity. Besides earning their livelihood in film, stage and TV, the Stooges were now into the field of merchandising, their funny faces splashed on the covers of hundreds of issues of comic books, on toys and on an endless array of merchandising items from bubble gum to punching bags. Their record career was expanding rapidly, with albums for several companies, and the top television shows continued to plead with the Stooges for guest appearances. The details of the many facets of this peak in the Stooges' careers are too numerous to mention but are spelled out to the nth degree in one of my previous books, *The Three Stooges Scrapbook*, which I co-authored with Jeff and Greg Lenburg.

Although the Stooges would continue on with their profession into the early seventies, 1962 was without question the high point for them as an American entertainment phenomenon. *The Three Stooges Meet Hercules* was their top moneymaker and the most successful effort of their more than 200 films made for Columbia. It was a year that Moe, Larry and

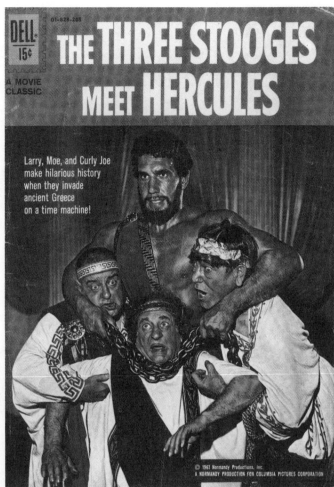

Three Stooges Meet Hercules *comic book, published by Dell.*

Officer Joe Bolton and his "Three Stooges Fun House," the Stooges' host on New York's TV station WPIX.

241

Curly-Joe would never forget as they moved on to make three more features for Columbia, continued cranking out TV films, sang up a storm on record albums, and had their far-out hair-dos immortalized in an unending array of merchandising items.

It is also a year that I shall never forget, as it started Norman on a career as a writer, producer and director at Columbia Pictures that was to last nine years.

Moe Howard's residence in 1962 in the Hollywood Hills.

The Chicago Tribune's *TV Magazine points up the Stooges resurgence during 1961.*

242

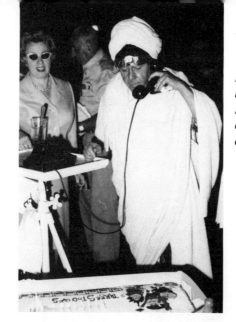

Moe's birthday cele-
brated on the set with
Helen as he takes a
congratulatory phone
call.

Norman, Moe, Helen, Mike and the author cele-
brating Moe's birthday, June 19, 1962.

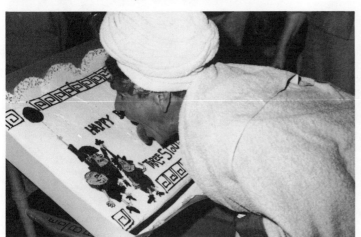

Moe lapping up a bit of cake Stooges style.

Moe reacts in surprise to his favorite
cake—chocolate with marshmallow icing.

Jeffrey, the author and Norman being given tour of
the Hercules *set by Stooge Moe.*

The Fine family visits the set. Row 1, on the right,
Larry's grandchild Kris Lamond, and son Johnny's
two children to the left, Row 2, Eric Lamond,
Larry, Phyllis and Don Lamond.

My brother Paul's wedding: (clockwise) Larry, Mabel, Joe DeRita, Phyllis Lamond (Larry's daughter), Don Lamond (Larry's son-in-law), Jeffrey and Michael Maurer (Moe's grandsons), Claretta White, Sam White (Jules White's brother), Norman Maurer, Joan Maurer, Bill Dyer.

1986

More Respect

PROCLAMATION

Three Stooges Day

WHEREAS, UCLA IS A MAJOR INSTITUTION OF HIGHER LEARNING IN THE CITY OF LOS ANGELES; AND

WHEREAS, THE UCLA FILM, TELEVISION & RADIO ARCHIVES IS ONE OF THE NATION'S LEADERS IN THE EFFORT TO PRESERVE FILM FOR HISTORICAL AND ARTISTIC PURPOSES; AND

WHEREAS, THE FILMS OF THE THREE STOOGES HAVE PROVIDED LAUGHTER AND JOY FOR MILLIONS OF PEOPLE, WORLDWIDE, DURING THE PAST 51 YEARS AND WILL CONTINUE TO DO SO FOR GENERATIONS TO COME; AND

WHEREAS, ON OCTOBER 25, 1985, COLUMBIA PICTURES INDUSTRIES, INC. IS DONATING A COLLECTION OF 190 THREE STOOGES SHORT SUBJECTS TO THE UCLA FILM, TELEVISION & RADIO ARCHIVES:

NOW, THEREFORE, I, TOM BRADLEY, MAYOR OF THE CITY OF LOS ANGELES, DO HEREBY PROCLAIM OCTOBER 25, 1985 AS "THREE STOOGES DAY" IN LOS ANGELES IN RECOGNITION OF THE CONTRIBUTION THE THREE STOOGES, COLUMBIA PICTURES INDUSTRIES, INC. AND UCLA FILM, TELEVISION AND RADIO ARCHIVES HAVE ALREADY MADE TO LOS ANGELES, AND TO THE BROADER CONTRIBUTION THEY WILL MAKE AS PROVIDERS AND PRESERVERS OF QUALITY ENTERTAINMENT MADE IN LOS ANGELES, WHICH REMAINS THE FILM CAPITAL OF THE WORLD BECAUSE OF THEIR WORK.

OCTOBER, 1985

Tom Bradley
MAYOR

245

Since *Book of Scripts—Volume I* was published in 1984, the fan letters, clippings and interesting stories regarding the steadfast and escalating popularity of the Stooges have continued to flow in and I have consistently tucked them into my file, on the off chance that I might be doing another book.

When the thought of respect and its relationship to the Three Stooges first came into my head, years ago, I asked myself the question, "Shouldn't the Three Stooges be included in the ranks of classic comedians?" The first thing I had to do before I could come up with an answer was run to the dictionary and look up the word classic. There I found the following definitions: 1. *Highest class.* (Well, that's out! The Stooges act both on and off stage was never considered "high class.") 2. *Basic, fundamental.* (Not quite "it" but I had the feeling I was getting warmer.) 3. *Enduring interest, quality and style.* (Now, that's more like it.) 4. *A work definitive in its field.* (Now there was the definition that hit the nail on the head and finally convinced me that the Three Stooges were indeed classic comedians.)

But this notion of mine was not always accepted by the media. In the early days of the Stooges' career, they were always left out when comedians were given any kind of tribute. It took many years of hard work and the efforts of an army of devoted fans before they were finally awarded their posthumous "star" on Hollywood's Walk of Fame. Critics also gave the Stooges short shrift; Chaplin, Laurel and Hardy, Buster Keaton and the Marx Brothers were the accepted, classic comedians while the Stooges were treated like poor relations—or worse yet, totally ignored.

There is little question that the circumstances which finally gave the Stooges the proper respect and equal status with the "masters of comedy" was the acceptance and love of a generation of "baby boom" fans who are still watching Stooges on television with their own youngsters sitting beside them. The "baby boomers" grew up with a five-day-a-week diet of Stooges Comedies and today look back with nostalgia on those happy days.

Violence was also a continuing problem for the Stooges which kept them from getting the respect they deserved. Today, however, with the saturated violence on television and in films, the Stooges' violence is often compared to that of animated cartoon characters such as Bugs Bunny and Wiley Coyote; their zany style of slapstick goes by unnoticed.

At present, the Stooges have not only respect but a degree of recognition that has surpassed all the comedians of their era. To illustrate my point, all one needs to do is draw three circles on a piece of paper, with the top half of one colored black to represent Moe's bangs, some squiggly circles at the top of another to represent Larry's frizzy hair and little gray dots representing Curly's shaven skull, and nine out of ten people will instantly recognize these simple circles as caricatures of the Three Stooges.

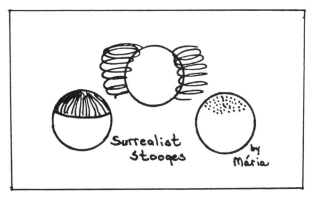

A perfect example of three simple circles that equal Three Stooges, by Maria Zulick.

Over the years, fans have continued to draw those simple, Stooges circles in more and more detail. One fan who demonstrated her respect for the Stooges, and my parents in particular, has become very dear to me. Her name is Belita Provenza William and she lived in Alhambra, California, back in the early sixties. One day she entered an art contest in which she had to draw a picture of the Stooges. The contest, sponsored by a local television station that aired the Stooges' shorts, awarded Belita first prize, which consisted of a badminton set and an interview with her favorite comedians. During the interview, Moe asked her to draw a picture of him and send it on. And what a surprise Moe had when he received it! Expecting a simple sketch, he was flabbergasted when Belita sent him a remarkable likeness of himself—a 36″ × 42″ oil painting in full color. And from that point on, Belita was like one of the family.

It is interesting to note what has happened to Belita as the years passed. A letter from her in 1979 brought me up to date on her art career. She wrote, "Well, good news. I was able to present my portrait of the King of Arabia (King Khalid) in person—which has only happened to one other American woman, I'm told. It was such an honor and I even met Crown Prince Fhad. Well, what do you think of that? Do you think your dad and mom (Moe and Helen) would have been proud of me? That means a lot as they had such faith in me."

Belita has kept in touch with my family over the years, and she and husband, Tony, and her five children are part of my inheritance from my father—wonderful fans and dear friends.

And it was those thousands of wonderful fans who contributed so mightily to the respect that the Stooges are receiving today. Week after week, my phone rings with a reporter from this newspaper, a radio or television host from that station, asking to interview me on the subject of the Stooges. Just this past week, I received a call from Jim Cohn, an old friend of Curly's from Bensonhurst, who put me in touch with Wally Phillips, a very popular Chicago talk-show host. Wally was a Stooges fan and wanted me on his show for a segment similar to the old TV series *I've Got a Secret*. My secret would be that Stooge Curly was my uncle.

Although I had never met either of the panelists who would question me—television talk show host Gary Deeb and actress-singer Kay Ballard—I was familiar with them and their careers. Gary, when he was a columnist for the *Chicago Sun-Times*, always spoke glowingly about the Stooges; and Kay Ballard, if I'm not mistaken, had played on the bill with the Stooges in vaudeville. The two had a difficult but fun time guessing my secret and broke into peals of laughter when they found out that kooky Curly was my uncle.

The second in my most recent Stooges tributes came today, in the form of a book of poems titled *Why Wait 'Til I'm Dead? Buy this Book Now!* by M. (Mike) Agrelius of Whittier, California. One of the poems in the book, titled "Dr. Howard, Dr. Fine and Dr. Howard," gave me quite a chuckle. For openers, the book has a very unusual dedication. It reads, "Dedicated to myself—because if I don't I may never get a book dedicated to me." In the fan letter which accompanied the book, Mike wrote, "Out of respect for (the Stooges) and the joy they have brought and continue to bring to so many generations, I wrote a poem for them and self-published a book, primarily so that this poem would be in print."

Although Stooges fans have always been tried and true down through the generations, the feelings of the press towards the Three Stooges, especially in 1985, have become more positive and continue to accelerate. The Stooges have had articles written about them or had their names dropped in every publication from *Playboy* to *Vogue*.

An item in the *Chicago Tribune* refers to the Stooges' careers as "slam-bang American fun."

And in the *Chicago Tribune* again on November 24, 1985, the Stooges received a very respectful tribute when the best-seller list in Chicago included the *Curly* book, sandwiched between Shirley McLaine's *Dancing in the Light* and Bob Hope's *Confessions of a Hooker*. Not bad for a Bensonhurst kid.

In Jim Healy's column in the Sports Section of the *Los Angeles Herald-Examiner*, he wrote: "Have the aura and allure of UCLA basketball faded so badly that even Three Stooges comedies, made more than 40 years ago in black and white, pack more appeal? 'Soitenly!' Curly would say—as 150,000 people watched basketball and 350,000 watched the Stooges."

In the May, 1986, issue of *Vogue* magazine, in a review of the popular French movie *3 Men and a Cradle*, the reviewer wrote: "A trio of swinging Paris bachelors turn into the Three Stooges when a baby is left on their doorstep."

In *USA Today*, Rich Scheinin's headline read, *"PARTIES BREAK PRESSURE BE-*

A portrait in oil of Moe by then 16-year-old artist Belita Provenza William (who went on to paint the portrait of the King of Saudi Arabia).

248

FORE EXAMS." The article went on to say, "Columbia University's Ivy Leaguers showed their smarts last weekend with a giant game of Simon Says and a Three Stooges film festival—plus parties and dancing to reggae music."

Comedian Jay Leno, who has always had a spot in his heart for Stooges, was quoted in *Playboy* Magazine, January, 1986, saying, "Take any guy from MIT with a doctorate in astrophysics, put him in front of a TV set. When Moe hits Larry in the face with a shovel, the guy will crack up. If you ever turn the Stooges on with a group of women in the room, they get hostile. Have you ever seen that list in *The People's Almanac* of the ten men most admired by men? There's Abraham Lincoln, Albert Einstein, Moe—."

And *Esquire* magazine with its "Dubious Achievements" for 1986 had a list titled "Reasons to go on Living in 1986," and mentioned "The forthcoming book *Curly—A Biography of the Superstooge.*" (I'll take this tongue-in-cheek mention any day of the week; that is, if they spell my name correctly, which they did.)

Then, in March of this year, I received a letter from Margaret Engel, staff writer for the *Washington Post*. She enclosed a clipping from the magazine section of her paper dated March 30th, written by Brad Lemley. It concerned his experiences at the Library of Congress where he goes at least twice a week. Lemley wrote, "The books are the library's main attraction, 21 million of them at recent count. I use them for research on free-lance stories and also insights into my personal, lifetime quest for Ultimate Meaning. I have also found many E-Z hamburger recipes. It is all there, from *Alfred North Whitehead's Symbolism, Its Meaning and Effect* to Joan Maurer's *Curly—An Illustrated Biography of the Superstooge.*"

One of the high points of 1985-1986 regarding respect was the ceremony at the Samuel Goldwyn Theatre of the Academy of Motion Picture Arts and Sciences. The Stooges on that night were, according to *Daily Variety* columnist Will Tusher, "notched up to cinematic art, marking Columbia Pictures' donation of the complete collection of 190 Three Stooges short subjects to the UCLA Film, Television & Radio Archives."

The event was emceed by film historian and critic Leonard Maltin, who 15 years ago wrote *Movie Comedy Teams*, which was the first book that recognized the special talents of the Three Stooges and their contribution to film comedy.

Edward Bernds, who directed 25 of the final Three Stooges short subjects, took the stage and said, "Their comic gifts eluded definition. I couldn't explain it a generation ago. I can't now."

As the ceremony continued, a succession of tributes came from performers and directors who worked with the Three Stooges and was climaxed by an accolade from Robert Rosen, director of the UCLA Archives, who accepted the formal presentation from Columbia Pictures' president Steve Sohmer. Sohmer then took the stage and his next words would have thrilled my father as they thrilled me.

"There really is good reason to take comedy seriously, and the Three Stooges in particular," said Sohmer as he described the "veritable cult status" the Stooges have attained and of their "whole new generation of fans." Mr. Sohmer closed his speech saying, "For 51 years the gorgeous Columbia lady has carried on a flaming love affair with the Three Stooges—and she's still carrying the torch for them today."

Also appearing on stage were Gary Owens, Emil Sitka, Rudy Vallee and Gail Storm (who made a 1945 Monogram feature with the Stooges). All had sincere words of respect for those three masters of mirth.

The evening ended with the presentation of a proclamation in which Los Angeles Mayor Tom Bradley declared October 25, 1985, Three Stooges Day in the city. Now I call that respect!

Greedy girl that I am, there is still one bit of respect missing which to my way of thinking is far more difficult to achieve than even the "Star" in the Walk of Fame, and like the campaign to get the Stooges their well-deserved "Star," it would take the combined efforts of Stooges fans everywhere to bring this campaign to fruition. This super-respectful challenge would be the appearance of the Stooges' portraits on a United States com-

Academy Night

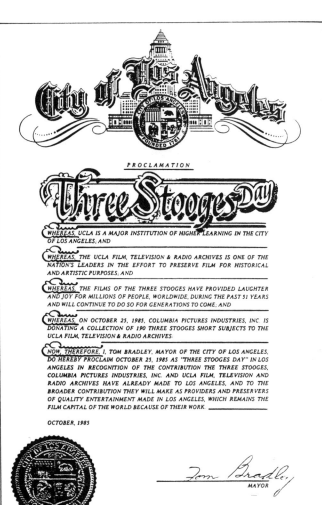

Photograph of mayor's proclamation.

The proclamation reads:

City of Los Angeles

PROCLAMATION

Three Stooges Day

WHEREAS, UCLA IS A MAJOR INSTITUTION OF HIGHER LEARNING IN THE CITY OF LOS ANGELES; AND

WHEREAS, THE UCLA FILM, TELEVISION & RADIO ARCHIVES IS ONE OF THE NATION'S LEADERS IN THE EFFORT TO PRESERVE FILM FOR HISTORICAL AND ARTISTIC PURPOSES; AND

WHEREAS, THE FILMS OF THE THREE STOOGES HAVE PROVIDED LAUGHTER AND JOY FOR MILLIONS OF PEOPLE, WORLDWIDE, DURING THE PAST 51 YEARS AND WILL CONTINUE TO DO SO FOR GENERATIONS TO COME; AND

WHEREAS, ON OCTOBER 25, 1985, COLUMBIA PICTURES INDUSTRIES, INC. IS DONATING A COLLECTION OF 190 THREE STOOGES SHORT SUBJECTS TO THE UCLA FILM, TELEVISION & RADIO ARCHIVES:

NOW, THEREFORE, I, TOM BRADLEY, MAYOR OF THE CITY OF LOS ANGELES, DO HEREBY PROCLAIM OCTOBER 25, 1985 AS "THREE STOOGES DAY" IN LOS ANGELES IN RECOGNITION OF THE CONTRIBUTION THE THREE STOOGES, COLUMBIA PICTURES INDUSTRIES, INC. AND UCLA FILM, TELEVISION AND RADIO ARCHIVES HAVE ALREADY MADE TO LOS ANGELES, AND TO THE BROADER CONTRIBUTION THEY WILL MAKE AS PROVIDERS AND PRESERVERS OF QUALITY ENTERTAINMENT MADE IN LOS ANGELES, WHICH REMAINS THE FILM CAPITAL OF THE WORLD BECAUSE OF THEIR WORK.

OCTOBER, 1985

Tom Bradley
MAYOR

Leonard Maltin (author and television personality).

The Columbia Pictures Industries Invitatio

Columbia Pictures Industries, Inc.
A subsidiary of *The Coca-Cola Company*

Columbia Pictures Industries, Inc. and
The UCLA Film, Television & Radio Archives
cordially invite you to a
Celebration of Comedy
in honor of the presentation of
The Three Stooges Collection to UCLA
Friday, October 25, 1985

The Academy of Motion Picture Arts and Sciences
8949 Wilshire Boulevard
Beverly Hills

7:30-8:30 PM	Reception
8:30 PM	Presentation
8:45 PM	Screening

RSVP (818) 954-3861

memorative stamp in 1990—the 60th Anniversary of their film career.

The Three Stooges
Commemorative Stamp

So why not start the ball rolling with a "STAMP FOR THE STOOGES" drive.

In 1987, Laurel and Hardy will have a very special honor bestowed upon them when they will be the subjects of a United States Commemorative Stamp.

Although this charming comedy team certainly deserves it, I would like to see if 1990 couldn't be the Stooges' year to stare out at us from the right-hand corner of envelopes and postcards. And why not? With their millions of fans and collectors of Stooges memorabilia, it just might be the government's biggest seller yet.

The odds may be against us—but then the odds were always against the "stooges." If each one of you could send a letter and find three or more fellow fans to send letters proposing the THREE STOOGES as subjects for a commemorative stamp, we just might beat those odds.

The year 1990 will be the 60th Anniversary of the Three Stooges' motion picture career which started in 1930 in the Fox film *Soup to Nuts* and ended with the comedy-travelogue *Kook's Tour* in 1970. During that period, the Stooges broke every record by starring in over 400 films. They certainly deserve the stamp not only for the quantity of films they made but for the joy and laughter they brought to three generations of Americans.

Incredible as it seems, the Stooges are still on television all over the world, and I defy you to go out on the street and take a poll of those persons who are currently watching the Stooges and those who are currently watching the "classic comedians," such as Chaplin, Laurel and Hardy and the Marx Brothers, and see what the answer will be.

I know we can make this very difficult challenge a reality and I desperately need your support; so grab your pen—and get to work. Send your letters to:

Citizen's Stamp Advisory Committee
c/o Stamps Development Branch
United States Postal Service
Customer Service Department
475 L'Enfant Plaza, SW
Washington, D.C. 20260–6300

Sheet of stamps from the Stooges 1959 Fan Club.

252

UNITED STATES POSTAL SERVICE
Customer Services Department
475 L Enfant Plaza, SW
Washington, DC 20260-6300

Dear Customer:

Thank you for your letter requesting information about the
stamp selection process.

We receive thousands of stamp proposals each year. They are
reviewed by the Citizens' Stamp Advisory Committee, whose
members are appointed by the Postmaster General from outside
the Postal Service according to their specialized knowledge.
The Committee is comprised of artists, historians, writers,
educators, stamp collectors and a representative of the
Treasury Department's Bureau of Engraving and Printing, where
most U.S. issues are manufactured. The Committee selects for
an average year 20 to 25 subjects to be developed fully and
presented to the Postmaster General for approval. Because of
the time required to print and distribute new issues, the
Committee makes its recommendations about two years in
advance of the proposed date of issuance.

I am enclosing a copy of the basic stamp selection
guidelines. You will note that there is no formal procedure
for submitting stamp suggestions. You need only to suggest
the subject and provide any background information you
believe would support the proposal.

We appreciate your interest in our stamp program.

                    Sincerely,

                    Hugh McGonigle
                    Philatelic Communications Specialist
                    Stamp Development Branch

Enclosure

Letter from the United States Post Office re Commemorative Stamps.

Citizen's Stamp Advisory Committee, guidelines.

Citizens' Stamp Advisory Committee
Issue Guidelines and Criteria
Page 2

Q: I have an idea for a commemorative stamp. How can I submit it
    for consideration?

A: Stamp subjects can be suggested by writing to the Citizens'
    Stamp Advisory Committee in care of the Stamps Development
    Branch.

    The selection of subjects for U.S. postage stamps is a
    difficult task, because only a limited number of new stamps
    are issued each year. To help in the selection of subjects,
    the Citizens' Stamp Advisory Committee has been established to
    consider the suggestions and recommend subjects and artists for
    various stamps. This committee is made up of historians,
    artists, businessmen, stamp collectors and others with keen
    interests in American history and culture. It is an advisory,
    body, and only the Postmaster General is empowered to approve
    on their recommendations.

    Stamp suggestions should take into account the following
    criteria established by the Citizens' Stamp Advisory
    Committee:

    ● No living person may appear on a U.S. postage stamp.
       With the exeception of recently-deceased Presidents, a
       person may be portrayed on a postage stamp 10 years after
       his or her death.

    ● Individuals are usually honored on significant
       anniversaries of their births.

    ● Significant historical events are considered for issuance
       on even-date anniversaries, preferably starting with
       their 50th year and continuing at 50-year intervals.

    ● Themes and events of widespread national appeal and
       significance are considered for postage stamps.

    ● In order to allow sufficient time for consideration by
       the Citizens' Stamp Advisory Committee and the necessary
       production processes, suggestions for stamps should be
       sent to the Postmaster General at least 36 months prior
       to the suggested date of issue.

While all you fans keep your letters coming in to the Post Office Department, I am going to ask Gary Owens to help with this drive as he did with the Stooges' "star," as well as write to radio stations, movie personalities and political figures.

Yes, a Commemorative Stooges Stamp could indeed be the ultimate in respect, and yet, somehow, I feel certain that my father, Larry and Curly would consider another form of respect just as important—and that is the never-ending stream of letters of devotion written by their fans. That's why I feel it appropriate to close this chapter on "Respect" by reprinting some of the letters and letting. . .

... The Fans Speak!

Artist: Richard Hoover.

THE FANS SPEAK:

Hello! My name is Chris. My friends are sick of hearing me say things about the Three Stooges. Could you please send me any kind of Stooge's memorabilia or a copy off a copy machine. I'm willing to pay for it. I'll even sign a contract. If you send me something I will either send you two corn holders or a screwdriver that I made in shop—or I'll send it even if you don't send me anything.

CHRIS BUHR *(address unknown)*

I'm 36 years old and I've been a devoted Stooges fan since Officer Joe Bolton first twisted his billy club on television. Somewhere in the seventies, the Stooges' shorts were nowhere to be found on the tube but, undaunted, I followed *Los Tres Chiflados* on Channel 47,

254

despite the fact that I don't understand a word of Spanish.

The books on comedy that I would pick up during the seventies made no reference to the Stooges. I shudder at those long battles with close-minded Laurel and Hardy and Abbott and Costello fans, but I stood strong. I remember the excitement when I found Leonard Maltin's book with a chapter on the Stooges; and I felt it was like a dream come true when I was told about Moe's biography. I could've sworn that the book had been written just for me.

TONY FRANCO, (West New York, New Jersey)

I have often suggested to people that Curly's name should be in the dictionary as the definition for the word "stooge." (A major publisher was one step ahead of you. In the 1960's printing of the *World Book Encyclopedia* there is a picture of all three Stooges and their names under "C" for Comedy.)

No rainy, dreary day could ever hope for a happier thought than the screening of a *Curly* two-reeler.

If I could answer the question: Who was a major influence for the better half of the twentieth century? I will say, firstly, Curly Howard— for all he has meant to every generation that grew up with his antics.

JOE CARUSO, (Cranford, New Jersey)

I am the president of my own corporation in New Jersey, and can be quite sophisticated and mature in any environment, but there is a big part of me—the Curly part—that's a fun-loving little boy that tries to be outrageous.

I'm going to be 40 next month but ever since I was old enough to understand television (around 8 years old), I loved the Three Stooges. In all this time my love hasn't diminished even an iota, and no matter how many times I may see the same episode (and I've seen them all many times) I never get bored. There is a quality about the Stooges' movies that I can't put my finger on.

MIKE WESTON, (Parsippany, New Jersey)

Rahst bonya yata bennie fuchi punya caronja yakaty-yakaty asky-tasky whattayou gotta here for froghead—and how are you? [That is exactly the way this fan letter started.]

I grew up in the 50's with the Stooges, yet I remain watching them still, into the 80's! It's something I don't need to understand—I just know I enjoy them. I felt that each Stooge possessed a unique ingredient in making up the perfect recipe for comedy. Many a time it was they who brought me out of depression and despair.

MIKE MODEJESKI, (Calumet City, Illinois)

[The following letter was not addressed to me but to my cousin Stanley. It is from his dear friend who is a professor at State University of New York]

"Thank you so much for my copy of *Curly*. After reading this book, I have a new appreciation for him, the Stooges, and you, my friend.

I did not realize the impact of the Three Stooges in 1985 until one of my students offered to buy my "Three Stooges Watch" right off my hand. (He offered a generous sum, which I, of course, refused.) The Stooges are being recognized and accepted by the après baby-boom generation. I am in awe.

My cousin Stanley's pride and joy, a Three Stooges Arcade Game, proudly displayed in his basement museum.

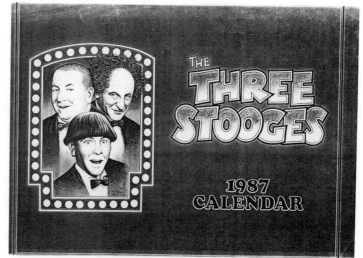

Three Stooges 1987 Calendar.

Most of all, the Curly biography makes me realize and understand your personal identification with Curly. Besides your common lust for life (food, drink and merriment) you are, like Curly, a solitary individual. Your generosities are comparable and your obsessions are similar.

The Curly book will sit on my coffee table as an honor to great comedy, a conversation piece of the 80's and a personal tribute to you."

ROBIN WAGNER, (Parkville, New York)

My "idea"—to make a long story short—is to cross the Stooges' likenesses with dogs in a comic strip. Now before you faint or die laughing, let me explain how this all came about.

In 1977, I had my first encounter with the Three Stooges in cartoon form. ("The Robonic Stooges"). I'd sit in front of the TV, sometimes laughing so loud I'd wake everyone up. I had no idea at the time that these silly guys were real.

From late 1979 into the mid-1980's, I was in a bit of a depressed state. It seemed everything I did was going wrong. You see, I'm the kind of person that could laugh at myself if I did something stupid but during this period of time, I didn't find anything funny.

On what I felt was the worst day of my life, I locked myself in a room and turned on the TV, switching the knob and thinking I'd find nothing interesting. But then something on one channel caught my eye. It was a rather chubby fellow, chasing a parrot across a courtroom with a mallet. The parrot flew over the jurors heads and each time he swung at the bird, he'd miss, knocking the jurors out cold! The man's two partners proved themselves to be just as nutty. Two more Stooges shorts followed and in that hour I was hooked, a Stooge fan for life. They made me do something I hadn't done in months—laugh. And I laughed so hard, I was in tears. Whoever said that laughter was the best medicine must've been describing a dose of the Three Stooges.

Being an artist, I tried to draw them, but since I was also terrible at drawing people, the only thing that came out right was their patented hair cuts. Disgusted, I stared at the scribbled attempts on my pad and drew Moe's hair cut once more. Then I thought to myself, "What's the best thing you can draw?" In-

Artist: Janet Gamble.

stantly I drew a dog's face under Moe's hair, then I did the same with Curly and Larry, and I've been doing so ever since.

JANET GAMBLE, (Brooklyn, New York)

NORMAN MAURER

While preparing this book for publication, Norman Maurer passed away on November 23, 1986 This was his last finished work.